Barry Sampson Teaching + Practice

Documents in Canadian Architecture

Dalhousie Architectural Press
Faculty of Architecture and Planning
Dalhousie University
Halifax, Nova Scotia, Canada
dal.ca/archpress

Barry Sampson: Teaching + Practice
Editors: Brian Carter and Annette LeCuyer
Designed by Christian Unverzagt at M1DTW
Typeset in Frutiger

Printed in Canada by Friesens on FSC certified GardaMatt Art text paper by Lectca and Kraft-Tone Carbon Copy Kraft cover paper made with 100% post-consumer recycled fiber and 100% renewable hydropower by French Paper Company.

Library and Archives Canada Cataloguing in Publication

Title: Barry Sampson: teaching + practice / Brian Carter and Annette LeCuyer, editors.
Names: Carter, Brian, editor. | LeCuyer, Annette W., editor.
Identifiers: Canadiana 20210253320 | ISBN 9780929112763 (softcover)
Subjects: LCSH: Sampson, Barry. | LCSH: Architects—Ontario—Toronto—Biography. | LCSH: College teachers—Ontario—Toronto—Biography. | LCSH: Architecture—Canada. | LCGFT: Biographies.
Classification: LCC NA749.S25 B37 2021 | DDC 720.92—dc23

Barry Sampson Teaching + Practice

Introduction

Richard Sommer 7

Baird Lecture

Barry Sampson 9

Practice

George Baird 76

Thomas L. Wells Public School 78

McEwen Graduate Study & Research Building 84

Jon Neuert 90

Teaching + Practice

Robert Wright	97
Brigitte Shim	98
Ian MacDonald	99
Pina Petricone	101
Erik Olsen	103
David Bowick	104
In Conversation: Richard Sommer & Nader Tehrani	106
Bruce Kuwabara	111
Donald McKay	112
John van Nostrand	114
Joost Bakker	116
Sampson Cottage	118
Contributors	124
Endnotes	127
Credits & Acknowledgements	128

Introduction

Richard Sommer

In the generations that followed the breakthrough modernist accomplishments of the early 20th century, many young architects were influenced by Le Corbusier's credo (and the title of his 1960 book) "creation is a patient search."[1] Barry Sampson came of age during this time, when many of the excesses of late modernism were also subject to a postmodern critique, when sometimes overlooked modernist figures like Alvar Aalto, and movements such as Russian Constructivism, were being re-evaluated and put to new purposes. This 'other' modernism was, architecturally speaking, Barry's starting point, and one can read the evolution of his work with George Baird, and later Baird Sampson Neuert, through this lens.

While I cannot recall Barry ever using Le Corbusier's coinage, his life as an architect and teacher, especially his practice of drawing to think, and his tendency to keep pushing and refining a project as far as it could be taken – whether a building design or a teaching brief – all speak to his passion and patience for the search. Alas, we do not live in a patient time. Whether the success one seeks is commercial and financial in kind, or more the kind that comes with the look of one's work gaining attention in the media – regardless of its reality on the ground – speed, efficiency, and canny market positioning are the rules of the day. In this sense, Barry never accepted those aspects of the intertwined postmodern and corporate bureaucratic turn in architecture that elevate image and expediency over substance.

Barry eschewed the contemporary path to easy success by committing himself to architectural (and other) values that are not immediately visible. By this I mean that he was looking for meaningful links between how architecture appears and how it performs – for example, the sound and touch of a building, and how it connects to its climate and environment. I was recently on a panel to review a proposed new masterplan for the University of Toronto Mississauga. The core of this campus is a 1970s brutalist concrete quasi-megastructure set within a forest. Typical of many contemporary campuses, Mississauga's expansion over time has produced a mishmash of planning gestures and architectures. As I looked at some of the new analyses and master planning proposals, I struggled with some of my colleagues to point to what was missing, something that could create a more coherent set of relationships between the campus's ad hoc mix of buildings, landscape, and infrastructure. I found myself focusing on one of the only buildings from the expansion of the campus that achieved such a synthesis – Baird Sampson Neuert's Erindale Hall. One of the firm's award-winning projects, led by Barry, this commodious student residence defines the boundary between a formal green and a wooded riparian zone, and formalizes an arcaded campus walk across its public face. Erindale Hall quietly illustrates how to craft an architecture out of seeming chaos, and is an embodiment of the idea that great works of architecture are not necessarily singular, but imply something larger by way of their extension or proliferation. Barry was a teacher and, like Erindale Hall, many of his projects were object lessons of this kind.

Barry Sampson was an example of how we can be ambitious, stay true to our values, and yet still remain open, kind and, most of all, generous of spirit. Like the architecture he pursued in practice and promoted as a teacher, Barry never sought undue attention, knowing that the most important things must sometimes happen behind the scenes. He was also frank about how much his own patient search made him subject to the often brutal realities and disappointments of practicing architecture. As the essays and remembrances contained in this book – and Barry's own words – attest, he managed it all with a sly and self-deprecating sense of humor, and still loved architecture, and being an architect and teacher, to the end. His faith is something I will keep and try to share.

Baird Lecture

Barry Sampson

Questions of Practice

George Baird Architect to Baird Sampson Neuert architects

I would like to thank Dean Sommer and the Faculty for inviting me to deliver the 2019 Baird Lecture. Thank you, George, for the kind introduction. I would also like to take this opportunity to thank my beloved partner Judi Coburn for her years of support throughout the period of work I am presenting, as well as my sons Benjamin and Martin Sampson-Coburn for teaching me about life, which should be, but has not always been, balanced with work. There are many other people – friends, students, teaching colleagues, professional colleagues – from whom I have learned more about civility, ideas, and practice than I could ever adequately acknowledge. As is the convention in publishing, I will say up front that any errors in the execution of this lecture are mine alone.

George Baird became a registered architect and a sole practitioner in 1969. In 1972, he expanded his practice to include four of his freshly graduated students, one of whom was me. In 1978, I left his firm for a sabbatical year in France, during which I intended to learn French and reflect on what I should do next with my career. George and I agreed to become partners in Paris in 1979, and we formed Baird Sampson Architects in 1981 after I completed my Ontario Association of Architects registration. In 1997, Jon Neuert became a principal, and the firm was incorporated as Baird Sampson Neuert architects. Jon had been a student of mine in the joint architecture/landscape architecture studio of the former Bachelor of Architecture Program at the University of Toronto and had been recruited to work on Cloud Gardens Park.

Towards the end of his life, Jean-Jacques Rousseau completed three writing tasks: the *Dialogues, The Confessions,* and *The Reveries of the Solitary Walker.*[1] The first endeavoured to explain to others what he had been trying to do through his work and actions. The second sought to explain to others and himself his behaviour based on the "naturalness" of his character. The last simply was a reflection, for himself, on the meaning of his actions and behaviour.

This lecture is a reflection that considers the work trajectory and motivations of an architectural and urban design firm over almost 50 years of practice. Although it is a less personal enterprise than Rousseau's, I like to think it merits similarly fundamental questions.

I have organized the lecture around five questions, one for each decade of the firm's practice. In my view, the first four have defined the ethos, direction, and work of the firm in very significant ways. The fifth addresses architectural practice in our contemporary context and remains an open question. It is my hope that students will find my discussion of these questions pertinent to questions they may have themselves about the practice of architecture. With this audience in mind, I have tried to privilege representations, drawn and digital, as students come to know their own work primarily in this way.

HELL
FOR
GIRLS

For Whom Do We Work?

Architecture is somewhat different than the fine arts in that a project is normally instigated by someone other than the architect – a client of some kind. While clients may well be inspiring "instigators," they are typically not the only "motivators" for the way the work is carried out and the precise form it takes. That inspiration can come from elsewhere and may determine the significance of the project's contribution to design culture. In our firm and the arc of its creative trajectory, the role of clients in defining the project's purpose has been balanced with other significant "motivators."

One cannot talk about instigators and motivators without also talking about constraints. One constraint is context; an architectural work is normally built in a place with its own form and history. Another is budget, the troublesome bed partner of the architect. In the case of an art project, the budget more than likely follows from the artistic idea and how it might be most fully realized.

If Henry Moore and his patrons could not have afforded a bronze caster, the *Archer* at Toronto's New City Hall would either not be there at all or would be another kind of artwork entirely. In the case of the architect, the budget typically comes first, along with a functional program, the accommodation of which is often the instigator of a client's pursuit of an architect.

Sometimes, projects are instigated by unanticipated events. The rebuilding of Dunbarton-Fairport United Church in Pickering, for example, was one of the first and largest building projects to come to our office. Don McKay, a friend of the firm, had an uncle who was a minister suddenly confronted by a big architectural problem when his church was badly damaged by fire.

The first manifestation of the firm, then called George Baird Architect, was photographed on a site analysis trip to Eglinton Avenue and Highway 401.

Our band of explorers included Joost Bakker, looking to the future; the irrepressible leader of the band, George Baird; the pantomiming motorcycle rider singing "Leader of the Pack" in his mind, Barry Sampson; and the project visionary, John van Nostrand. This group – which also included Bruce Kuwabara, the photographer outside the frame – was preparing a design submission for the international design competition "The City as a Significant Environment," sponsored by *Casabella* magazine. In this case, the project instigator was an open international competition, but the motivator was the potential it offered to make a major design statement about new forms of suburban infrastructure and public space development. The band came together to do such competitions and intended to use the amplification of John van Nostrand's fifth-year thesis as a competition entry, as well as an armature to explore what the group could possibly achieve working together. Of course, this was only the first step to achieving world design domination.

Academic Bookshop,
Alvar Aalto, 1962

Also missing from the photo of the band is Elizabeth Baird who, with George, played a remarkable role in hosting many dinners and socials at their wondrous attic apartment on Hogarth Avenue. These events kept the band members well fed, despite a paucity of professional fees, and they also provided an exceptional diet of social and cultural discourse. On a number of occasions, those discussions included visiting architectural notables, including James Stirling, Arata Isozaki, Kenneth Frampton, and others.

The photo represents our collective desires and creative predilections. As a group, we shared a pantheon of heroes and heroic projects that provided benchmarks and motivators for high-level work. Similarly, each individual possessed his own set of heroes and reference projects that defined problems of design in meaningful ways.

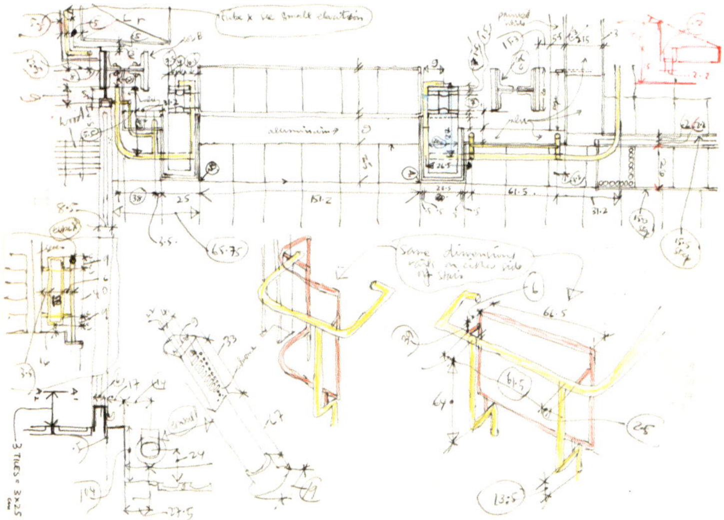

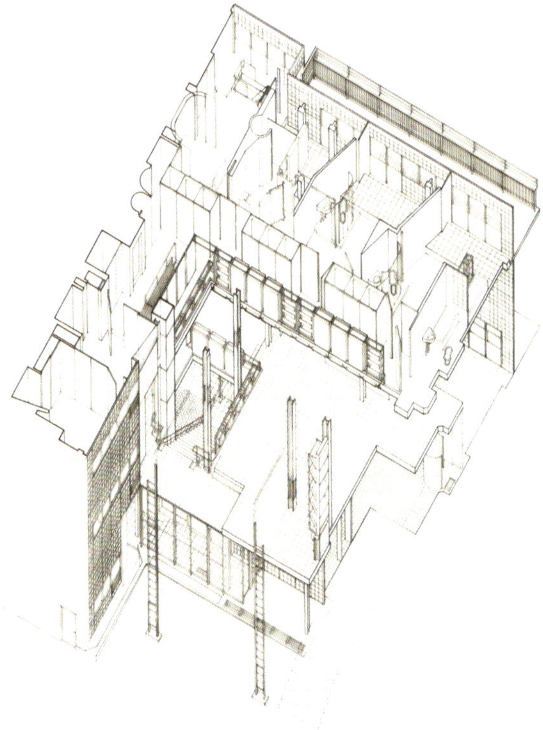

Maison de Verre,
Pierre Chareau and Bernard Bijvoet, 1932

Field sketches and axonometric,
Kenneth Frampton for *Perspecta 12*

George Baird had just published his book on Alvar Aalto.[2] He also brought *Perspecta 12* to the attention of the group. In this 1969 edition of The Yale Architectural Journal, Kenneth Frampton documented and analyzed the Maison de Verre.[3] For me, this project by Pierre Chareau and Bernard Bijvoet was a revelation – an idea of modern life, and audacious detailing to match. At the time, I was interested in the conceptual problem of architecture as a modern form of building.

Schroeder House,
Gerrit Rietveld, 1924

Like Chareau, Gerrit Rietveld started out as a cabinet maker. Although not a theorist himself, he designed what came to be seen as representative projects of "elementarism" advocated by Theo van Doesburg, the best-known theorist of the De Stijl movement. The preponderance of vertical and horizontal planes characterizing many towers on the Toronto skyline today is evidence of how deeply elementarism became embedded in the DNA of modernism.

My colleagues and I were also admirers of the Constructivist movement, which married revolutionary form making with revolutionary politics. As Gary Michael Dault proclaimed to one of my first-year studio classes in the Sharon Temple, the Constructivists took architecture off the X and Y axes to create dynamic imbalance. Rem Koolhaas, in his 1972 thesis at the Architectural Association in London, "Exodus, or the voluntary prisoners of architecture," made both formal and rhetorical references to that same movement.[4]

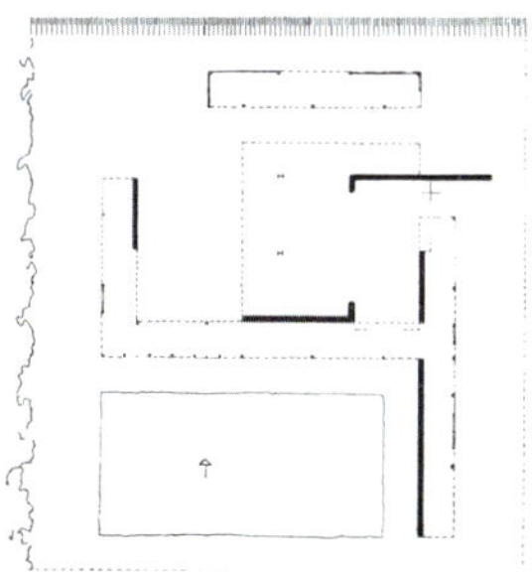

Sculpture Pavilion,
Gerrit Rietveld, 1955
(rebuilt 1965 and 2010)

Film Studio competition,
Ivan Leonidov, 1927

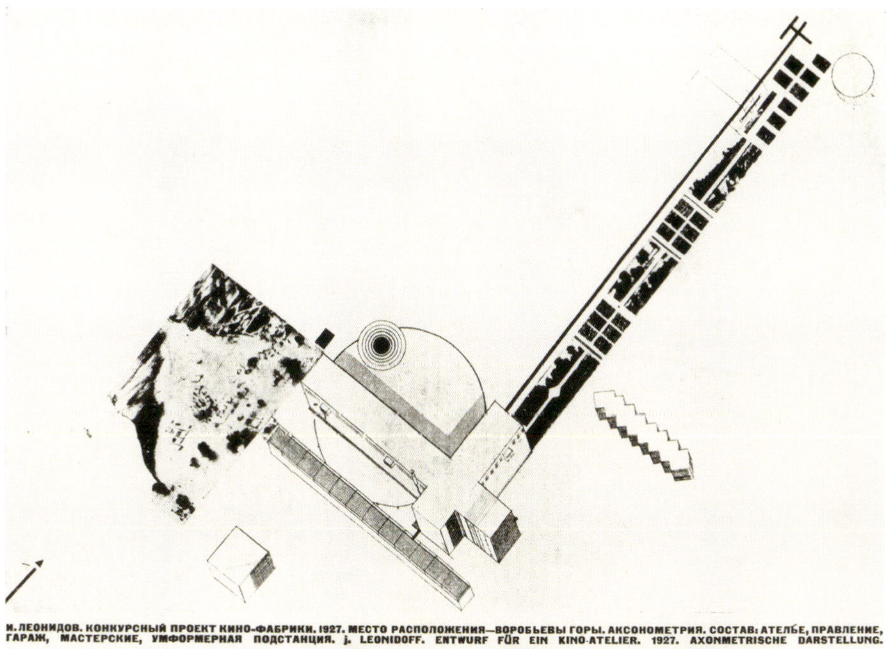

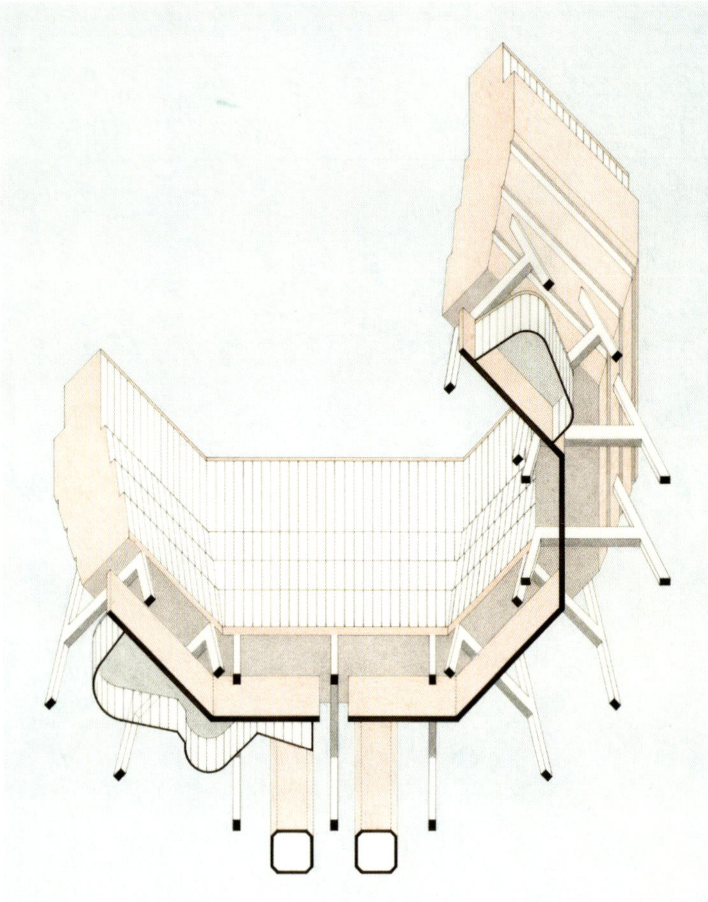

Florey Building, Queen's College, Oxford, James Stirling, 1971

The work of James Stirling became an ongoing touchstone of the firm for a number of reasons. First, in the early days we mostly drew projects, and Stirling and Gowan's work was exemplary in the use of intelligent drawing to convincingly convey design ideas. This was most clearly articulated by Don McKay, whom I think of as our Eric Clapton character – a talented supportive friend, who was around the band in the early days, joined it for a brief period, and then went off do his own thing. Stirling's inventive work with patent glazing systems was also inspiring for its creative form making using inexpensive technology. Finally, we could see and were inspired by the development of a critical practice in Stirling's work vis-à-vis modernism and the evolution of its own history.

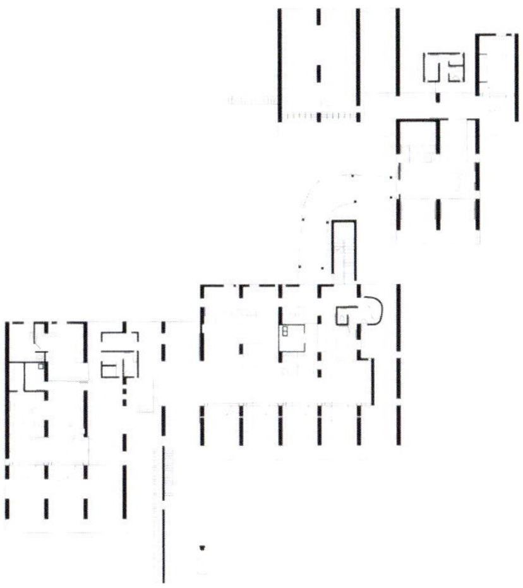

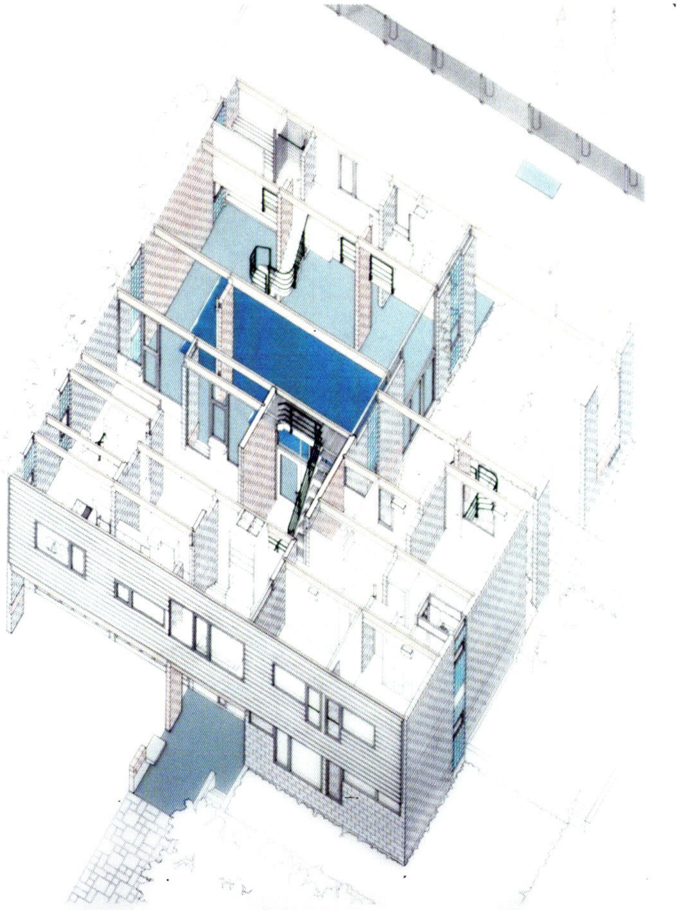

Sculpture Pavilion,
Aldo van Eyck, 1966
(rebuilt 2006)

Sarabhai House,
Le Corbusier, 1955

The axonometric of the Amalraj House project drawn by Bruce Kuwabara has its own idea, but one can see precedents in the pattern of concrete block walls of Aldo van Eyck's Sonsbeek Sculpture Pavilion and the rigorous cross-wall pattern with syncopated openings of Le Corbusier's Sarabhai House. Unfortunately, the Amalraj House was not built as designed. The client was persuaded by another architect, who happened to also be a contractor, to build it in a more conventional manner out of brick. George resigned the commission at that point as a matter of personal design integrity, bringing us, early on, face to face with the question "For whom do we work?"

An article that Bruce Kuwabara and I wrote for *City Magazine* in 1975 was reprinted in *The City Book* in 1976, both published by James Lorimer & Co.[5] By that time, the forms and planning ideas of heroic modernism had been

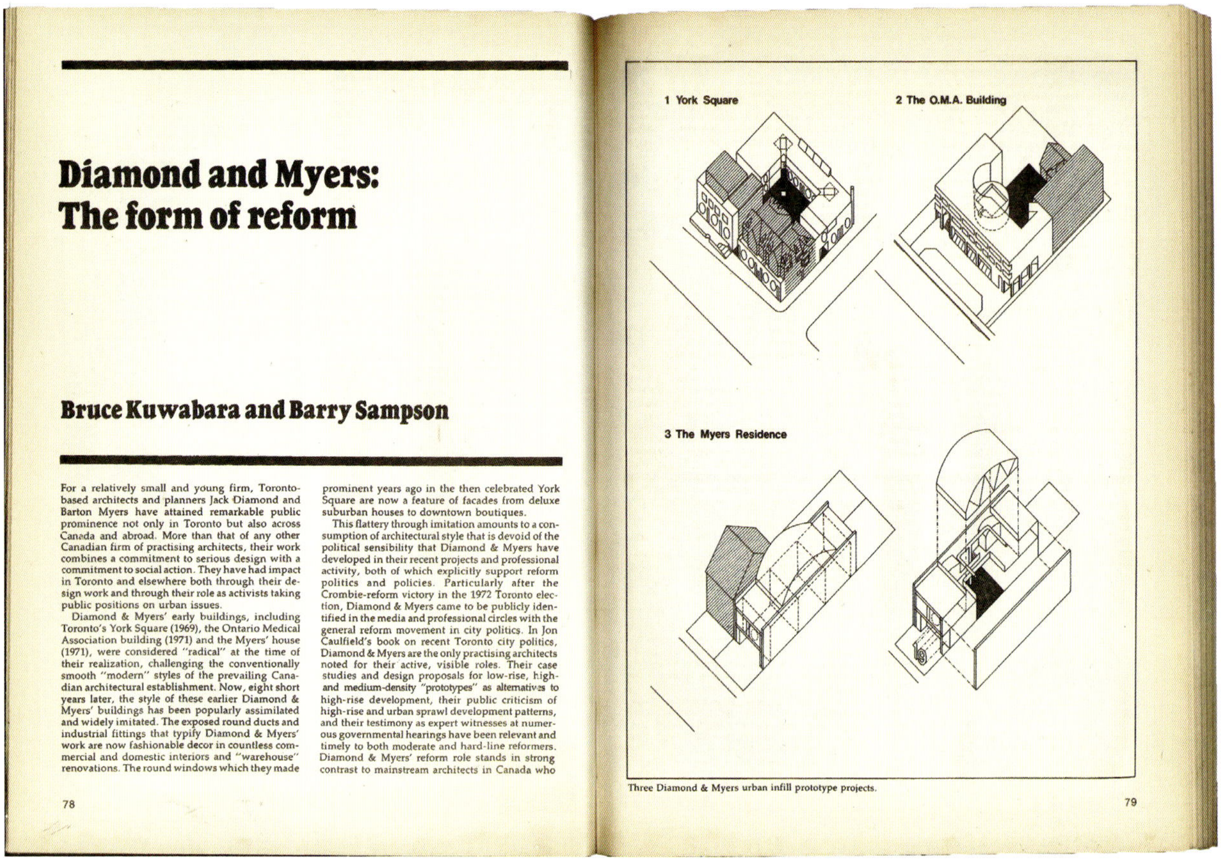

Diamond and Myers: The form of reform

Bruce Kuwabara and Barry Sampson

For a relatively small and young firm, Toronto-based architects and planners Jack Diamond and Barton Myers have attained remarkable public prominence not only in Toronto but also across Canada and abroad. More than that of any other Canadian firm of practising architects, their work combines a commitment to serious design with a commitment to social action. They have had impact in Toronto and elsewhere both through their design work and through their role as activists taking public positions on urban issues.

Diamond & Myers' early buildings, including Toronto's York Square (1969), the Ontario Medical Association building (1971) and the Myers' house (1971), were considered "radical" at the time of their realization, challenging the conventionally smooth "modern" styles of the prevailing Canadian architectural establishment. Now, eight short years later, the style of these earlier Diamond & Myers' buildings has been popularly assimilated and widely imitated. The exposed round ducts and industrial fittings that typify Diamond & Myers' work are now fashionable decor in countless commercial and domestic interiors and "warehouse" renovations. The round windows which they made prominent years ago in the then celebrated York Square are now a feature of facades from deluxe suburban houses to downtown boutiques.

This flattery through imitation amounts to a consumption of architectural style that is devoid of the political sensibility that Diamond & Myers have developed in their recent projects and professional activity, both of which explicitly support reform politics and policies. Particularly after the Crombie-reform victory in the 1972 Toronto election, Diamond & Myers came to be publicly identified in the media and professional circles with the general reform movement in city politics. In Jon Caulfield's book on recent Toronto city politics, Diamond & Myers are the only practising architects noted for their active, visible roles. Their case studies and design proposals for low-rise, high- and medium-density "prototypes" as alternatives to high-rise development, their public criticism of high-rise and urban sprawl development patterns, and their testimony as expert witnesses at numerous governmental hearings have been relevant and timely to both moderate and hard-line reformers. Diamond & Myers' reform role stands in strong contrast to mainstream architects in Canada who

78

Three Diamond & Myers urban infill prototype projects.

79

appropriated by capitalism. To achieve these ideas more systematically, the mantra of "comprehensive redevelopment" became embedded in city planning codes and practices. The result was conflict with the historic city, as predatory redevelopment projects erased groupings of heritage structures downtown and took apart established neighbourhood patterns. The relatively young architectural firm Diamond and Myers played a key role in critiquing such practices, while also creating a portfolio of signature work. Our article was an endeavour to understand what that approach could mean as a model for a new kind of critical practice.

In the 1981 book *After the Developers,* Lorimer also published an article entitled "Main Street: Can it Survive the Shopping Centre?" that George Baird and I authored, which summarized research and analysis we had done on redevelopment crises being experienced by mid-sized towns in Ontario.[6]

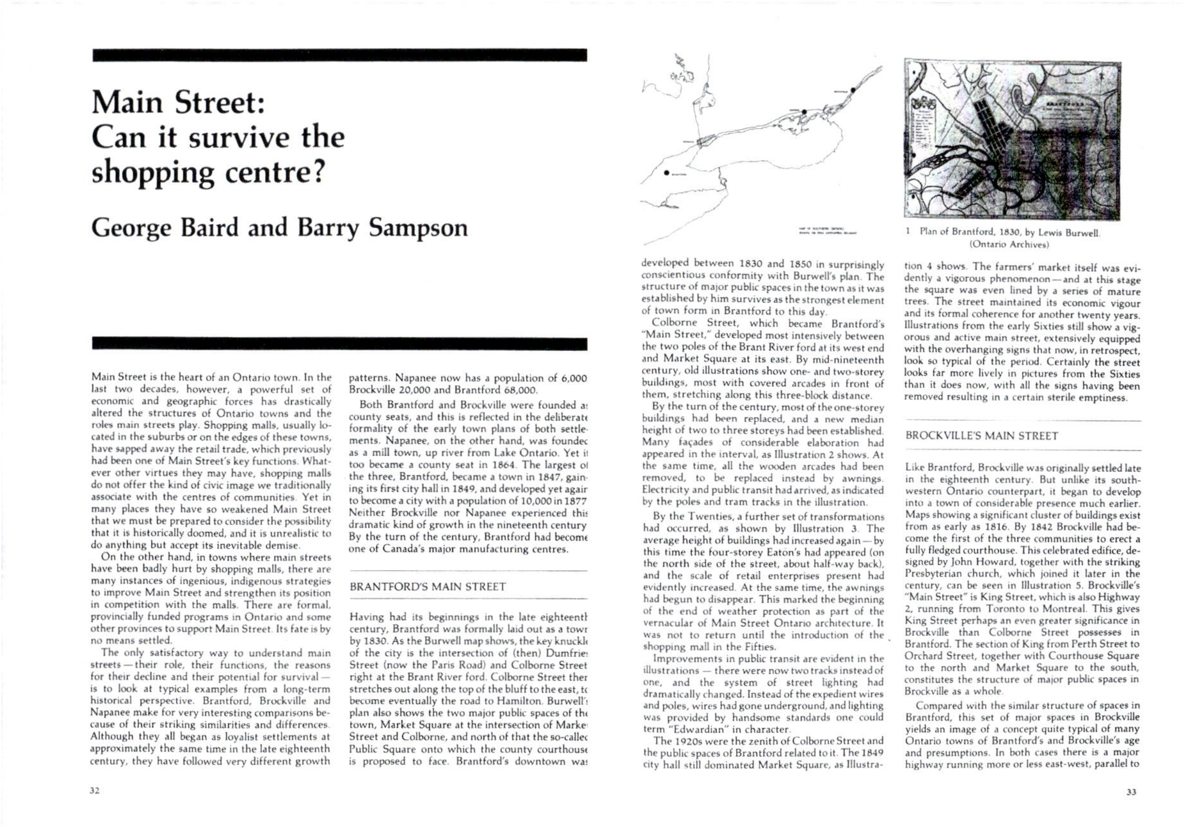

Main Street: Can it survive the shopping centre?

George Baird and Barry Sampson

Main Street is the heart of an Ontario town. In the last two decades, however, a powerful set of economic and geographic forces has drastically altered the structures of Ontario towns and the roles main streets play. Shopping malls, usually located in the suburbs or on the edges of these towns, have sapped away the retail trade, which previously had been one of Main Street's key functions. Whatever other virtues they may have, shopping malls do not offer the kind of civic image we traditionally associate with the centres of communities. Yet in many places they have so weakened Main Street that we must be prepared to consider the possibility that it is historically doomed, and it is unrealistic to do anything but accept its inevitable demise.

On the other hand, in towns where main streets have been badly hurt by shopping malls, there are many instances of ingenious, indigenous strategies to improve Main Street and strengthen its position in competition with the malls. There are formal, provincially funded programs in Ontario and some other provinces to support Main Street. Its fate is by no means settled.

The only satisfactory way to understand main streets — their role, their functions, the reasons for their decline and their potential for survival — is to look at typical examples from a long-term historical perspective. Brantford, Brockville and Napanee make for very interesting comparisons because of their striking similarities and differences. Although they all began as loyalist settlements at approximately the same time in the late eighteenth century, they have followed very different growth patterns. Napanee now has a population of 6,000 Brockville 20,000 and Brantford 68,000.

Both Brantford and Brockville were founded as county seats, and this is reflected in the deliberate formality of the early town plans of both settlements. Napanee, on the other hand, was founded as a mill town, up river from Lake Ontario. Yet it too became a county seat in 1864. The largest of the three, Brantford, became a town in 1847, gaining its first city hall in 1849, and developed yet again to become a city with a population of 10,000 in 1877. Neither Brockville nor Napanee experienced this dramatic kind of growth in the nineteenth century. By the turn of the century, Brantford had become one of Canada's major manufacturing centres.

32

BRANTFORD'S MAIN STREET

Having had its beginnings in the late eighteenth century, Brantford was formally laid out as a town by 1830. As the Burwell map shows, the key knuckle of the city is the intersection of (then) Dumfries Street (now the Paris Road) and Colborne Street right at the Brant River ford. Colborne Street then stretches out along the top of the bluff to the east, to become eventually the road to Hamilton. Burwell's plan also shows the two major public spaces of the town, Market Square at the intersection of Market Street and Colborne, and north of that the so-called Public Square onto which the county courthouse is proposed to face. Brantford's downtown was developed between 1830 and 1850 in surprisingly conscientious conformity with Burwell's plan. The structure of major public spaces in the town as it was established by him survives as the strongest element of town form in Brantford to this day.

Colborne Street, which became Brantford's "Main Street," developed most intensively between the two poles of the Brant River ford at its west end and Market Square at its east. By mid-nineteenth century, old illustrations show one- and two-storey buildings, most with covered arcades in front of them, stretching along this three-block distance.

By the turn of the century, most of the one-storey buildings had been replaced, and a new median height of two to three storeys had been established. Many façades of considerable elaboration had appeared in the interval, as Illustration 2 shows. At the same time, all the wooden arcades had been removed, to be replaced instead by awnings. Electricity and public transit had arrived, as indicated by the poles and tram tracks in the illustration.

By the Twenties, a further set of transformations had occurred, as shown by Illustration 3. The average height of buildings had increased again — by this time the four-storey Eatön's had appeared (on the north side of the street, about half-way back), and the scale of retail enterprises present had evidently increased. At the same time, the awnings had begun to disappear. This marked the beginning of the end of weather protection as part of the vernacular of Main Street Ontario architecture. It was not to return until the introduction of the shopping mall in the Fifties.

Improvements in public transit are evident in the illustrations — there were now two tracks instead of one, and the system of street lighting had dramatically changed. Instead of the expedient wires and poles, wires had gone underground, and lighting was provided by handsome standards one could term "Edwardian" in character.

The 1920s were the zenith of Colborne Street and the public spaces of Brantford related to it. The 1849 city hall still dominated Market Square, as Illustration 4 shows. The farmers' market itself was evidently a vigorous phenomenon — and at this stage the square was even lined by a series of mature trees. The street maintained its economic vigour and its formal coherence for another twenty years. Illustrations from the early Sixties still show a vigorous and active main street, extensively equipped with the overhanging signs that now, in retrospect, look so typical of the period. Certainly the street looks far more lively in pictures from the Sixties than it does now, with all the signs having been removed resulting in a certain sterile emptiness.

1 Plan of Brantford, 1830, by Lewis Burwell. (Ontario Archives)

BROCKVILLE'S MAIN STREET

Like Brantford, Brockville was originally settled late in the eighteenth century. But unlike its south-western Ontario counterpart, it began to develop into a town of considerable presence much earlier. Maps showing a significant cluster of buildings exist from as early as 1816. By 1842 Brockville had become the first of the three communities to erect a fully fledged courthouse. This celebrated edifice, designed by John Howard, together with the striking Presbyterian church, which joined it later in the century, can be seen in Illustration 5. Brockville's "Main Street" is King Street, which is also Highway 2, running from Toronto to Montreal. This gives King Street perhaps an even greater significance in Brockville than Colborne Street possesses in Brantford. The section of King from Perth Street to Orchard Street, together with Courthouse Square to the north and Market Square to the south, constitutes the structure of major public spaces in Brockville as a whole.

Compared with the similar structure of spaces in Brantford, this set of major spaces in Brockville yields an image of a concept quite typical of many Ontario towns of Brantford's and Brockville's age and presumptions. In both cases there is a major highway running more or less east-west, parallel to

33

Again, the motivation of our work was critical engagement with discourse on the quality of the public realm, beyond the architect's normal professional "duty of care" – engagement that we saw as our civic duty.

By this time, several members of our original band had departed for other opportunities: Joost Bakker moved to Vancouver, where he would partner with Norm Hotson to form Hotson Bakker and, more recently, DIALOG; Bruce Kuwabara went to Barton Myers Architect, from which he would found KPMB with Marianne McKenna, Shirley Blumberg, and Tom Payne; and John van Nostrand moved first to Hamilton, then back to Toronto to form his own firm, SvN Architects + Planners. George and I collaborated with John once again in 1996 on the Seaton New Town design competition.

Can Modernism Move Forward by Looking Back?

The heroic period of modernism eschewed historicity as part of a strategy to defeat slavish repetition of past styles associated with the repressive history and mores of the 19th century and pre-First World War era. By the '60s and '70s, questions of the inadequacy of this sensibility to address social and cultural problems of urbanism and the historic city were fuelling many theoretical discussions. Popular disaffection with what the "modern project" had become, when emptied of its original utopian and reformist social morale, blew up into the existential crisis typically referred to in architectural circles as postmodernism.

While the late work of James Stirling would eventually fall into the postmodernist camp, his mid-period work represented a new kind of critical modern practice that was historically engaged. The Leicester University Engineering Building was representative of a new way to look back at modernism's own history.

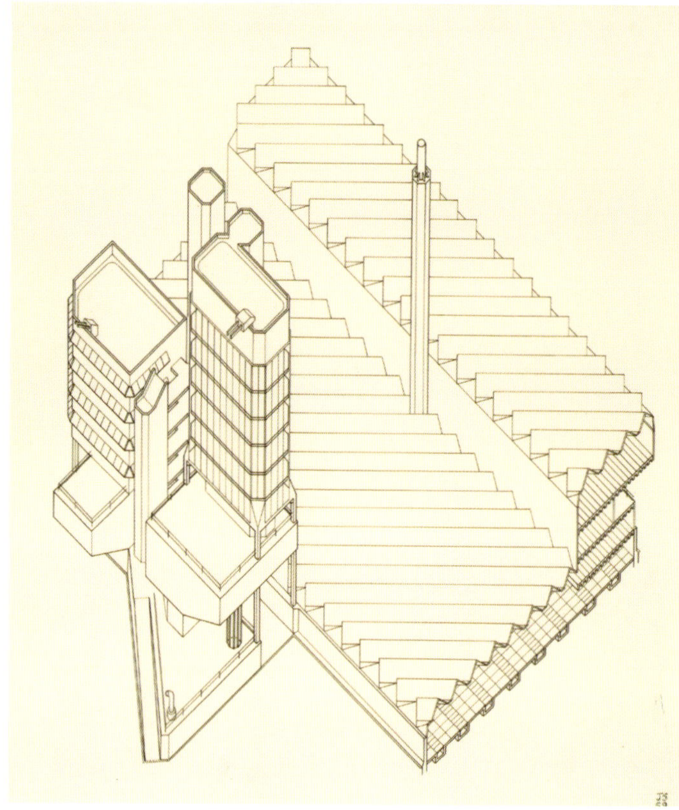

Leicester University Engineering Building, Stirling and Gowan, 1963

The Constructivist workers' clubs were captured in the circular stair. This scheme also presented what I would describe as a collagist approach to form and program that was deliberately anti-Platonic by eschewing the idealized unitary object as perfected by heroic modernists, notably Mies van der Rohe.

During my sabbatical in Paris, George Baird and I agreed to form Baird Sampson Architects. After I returned from France, the first major project the new partnership undertook was the Edmonton City Hall competition. Martin Kohn was working with us at the time as a member of our design team. Before commencing design, we visited Edmonton to analyze the site. The original modernist city hall – which we discovered was creatively contextual in the way its angled faces incorporated geometry derived from the angles of adjacent streets – is embedded in our entry. This splayed pattern was, in turn, a record of

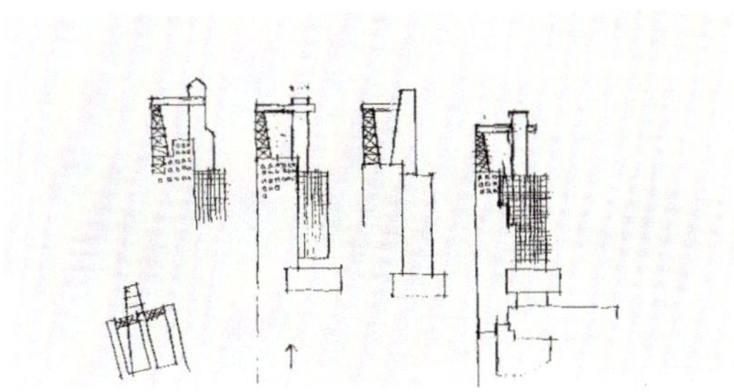

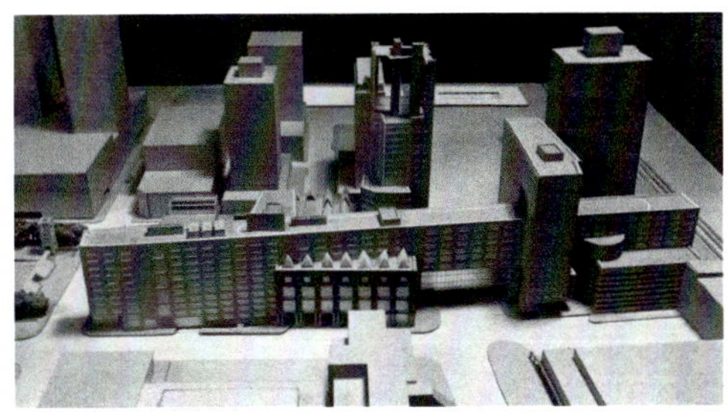

the historic river-based settlement pattern. It was a condition of the competition that the city hall from the '60s be cleared from the site – a condition we thought was culturally destructive. We decided to respond to this requirement by proposing to demolish and then reconstruct the original building.

We did not win the competition. However, our scheme generated considerable interest in architectural circles across the country. What remains important to me is the way the project collaged together formal elements that were emblematic of various functions of government in order to break the vast program down into a knowable civic terrain for social interchange and political action. George explored this new formal strategy with sketches of a civic tower that eschewed commercial tower tropes to make a public viewing gallery that embraced the city's prairie setting and served as a civic beacon.

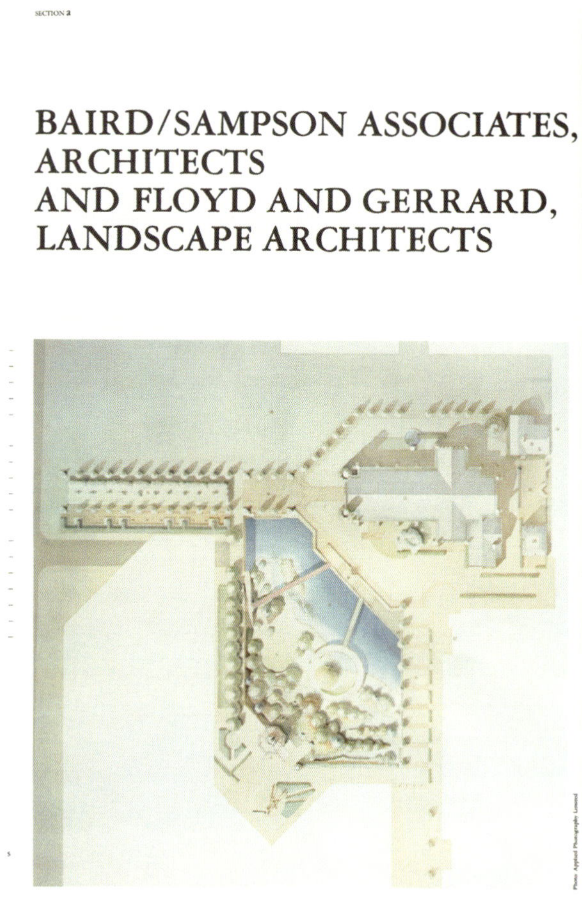

Although we failed to even place in the Edmonton competition, we were subsequently invited to participate in a design competition in Toronto for Trinity Square Park, located next to the Eaton Centre and encompassing the historic Trinity Church. Brigitte Shim was working in our office at the time and was on the design team; Howard Sutcliffe and John Soules helped with drawings. We knew the history of the site and the fact that Taddle Creek, which is now only visible as a valleyscape cutting through the University of Toronto, was enclosed in a storm sewer under the site. We thought the excavation and exposure of the creek's primordial condition would constitute a great design dialectic between a submerged picturesque landscape and an urban square at grade, with the church as its focus.

To bind these two experiences, we proposed a new tower spiralling down from grade and up to a gallery from which one would get a prized view and understanding of the layered history of the city. Once again, our scheme garnered attention for its originality, but it also generated controversy about how it would work as new kind of public space. Would it be safe? Would it attract the homeless? A more traditional design for the square, by a team headed by Ron Thom, was selected as the winner.

Our notoriety from the Trinity Square competition got us an invitation to participate in the design competition for a new public park to be built as a City of Toronto condition of approval of the Bay Adelaide commercial development. The site context of what was to become Cloud Gardens was innovative and unique: the park was to be on air rights owned by the City that extended

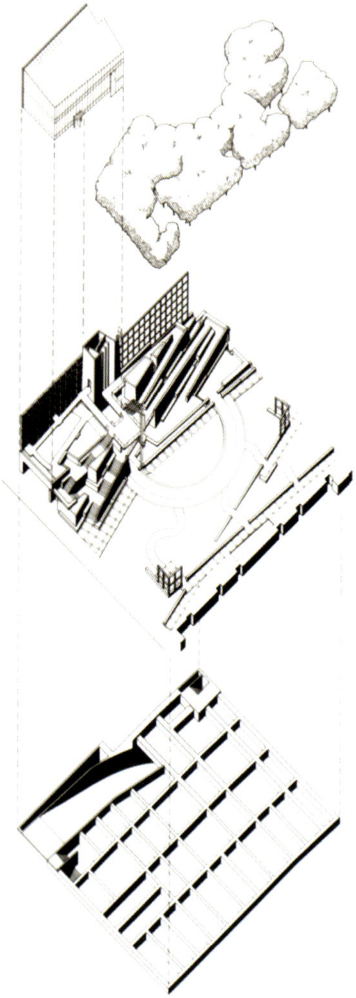

five feet below grade, above a food court and parking garage owned by the developer. Located a building lot depth west of Yonge Street and stretching between Richmond and Temperance Streets, the park was to be bracketed by a large-floor plate commercial tower to the south and a smaller mixed-use tower to the west.

Our site analysis indicated that the hyper-dense urban context of the park would block the sun to much of the ground area, and that daylight would become more available as one moved up in space. There was also a problem posed by an urban scar on the east side of the park where unfinished party walls had been exposed by demolition. The obvious design solution seemed to be the opposite of our Trinity Square approach: make a rising topography. A ramped terrain and terraces were proposed to mask the scar and create

places for sitting in the sun. This also allowed us to reclaim space over the parking garage entry and the exit stairs of the underground development. Our team included artists Margaret Priest and Tony Scherman, as well as landscape architects Milus Bollenberg Tops Watchorn. The competition brief invited the inclusion of a monument to construction workers, which Margaret Priest designed beautifully as sample panels fabricated by various construction trades.

At the time of the competition, downtown Toronto was in the midst of a cyclical real estate boom and cranes dotted the skyline. The design imagined the entire park as a critical monument to the process of construction, demolition, and reconstruction. However, no city builder is more capricious than human history itself. The real estate boom collapsed, and the park and underground facilities were the only parts of the original development project actually built.

The irony of history continues. A new owner of the site, Brookfield Developments, resumed building south of Cloud Gardens a number of years ago, constructing two towers instead of a single fat tower. They recently received planning approval from the City to build a tall third tower on the western edge of the park and to demolish half of the soft landscape to provide a staging area for its construction. This recent permission also includes the condition that the original park be "reinstated" after construction. We hope this will mean restoration of the original design intent.

How Could Architecture Respond to both Weather and Biological Needs?

Cloud Gardens Park received a Governor General's Award, was published internationally, and became a popular site for film shoots and events. It also opened doors to larger architectural projects for the firm. Our scheme included a glass enclosed wintergarden that attracted the interest of the Niagara Parks Commission, which wanted to build a butterfly conservatory at its Botanical Garden and Horticulture School. This project precipitated, in a major way, the question of how architecture could respond to both weather and biological needs. This seems like a simple enough question. Of course, buildings must be responsive to weather; they need to keep the rain and cold out. Furthermore, they have to provide interior environments appropriate to accommodating the biological needs of inhabitants comfortably, safely, and congenially.

However, designing the largest and most northerly glass display house for live butterflies in North America was a different challenge than a conventional building, not to mention the added task of incorporating rearing facilities for plants and caterpillars. We began researching insect entomology and what would be needed to make a successful artificial environment for live display. If there is not enough daylight, butterflies roost and do not fly. The environment needs to be relatively warm and humid, which creates the risk of significant condensation on glass, especially on cold nights. Butterflies rely on nectar, but in their caterpillar phase their food needs are completely different and they eat plants. Even though each butterfly species has its food preferences, they are biologically attuned to be adaptable and can quickly consume the landscape in a display house.

Simultaneously, we explored high performance greenhouse technology and how to incorporate weather-responsive passive ventilation and temperature control systems to minimize energy consumption. In addition, unlike the greenhouse industry that meets farm codes, this butterfly conservatory had to meet Ontario Building Code standards for assembly occupancy, so we had to figure out how to hybridize active greenhouse envelope technology with more robust conventional skylight glazing. Furthermore, the integration of other forms of active building technology, such as hydronic heating, with the architectonic form of a fundamentally light and transparent envelope required a high-level understanding of technical systems. These are considerations that architects normally, and happily, delegate to their engineering consultants.

Terror of failure is a great motivator. The level of rigour in design and detailing that our small team achieved over 25 years ago, at a time when digital modelling was in its infancy, is a tribute to their creative problem-solving abilities and dedication. The Butterfly Conservatory, which opened in 1996, was immediately a great success, with 750,000 visitors in its first year of operation. This intensity of use was a surprise to our client but not to Brian Arnott, a cultural facility management consultant on our team who helped us think through programming and facility operation needs. However, the energy performance of the building was a surprise, in that it consumed less energy in winter than anticipated. When we looked into why, we learned that the tons and tons of rock we had used to form durable landscape beds and a waterfall worked in concert with the greenhouse effect of the glass to create a heat sink that re-radiated stored solar energy at night.

The Butterfly Conservatory, which began as an exciting design challenge, became a primer for the firm on bioclimatic design and the first principles of high-performance environmentally responsive buildings. This was long before the popularization of LEED and other such green design protocols. This project also opened doors to new opportunities.

The Toronto District School Board commissioned Baird Sampson Neuert to design Thomas L. Wells Public School, its first green school. Typical of our working method, at the outset we embarked on research to better understand precedents and the project task. We learned that students perform significantly better in spaces that are daylit, rather than artificially lit, and that have good acoustic control. We then started to design this school from first principles of bioclimatic design, which led us to a number of innovations in the deployment of integrated systems.

We also worked with Toronto District School Board teachers and administrators as well as neighbourhood representatives to design the school as a place of community learning. For example, the special education room was integrated into the library, where it is suspended like a tree house. For the gym, we argued for and received permission to break convention, glazing the exterior wall in order to open events inside to the street. We experimented with the design of roof monitors to achieve effective daylighting with no glare in the areas of play. In addition, automated vents using greenhouse technology were integrated into the glazed faces of the monitors to provide natural ventilation.

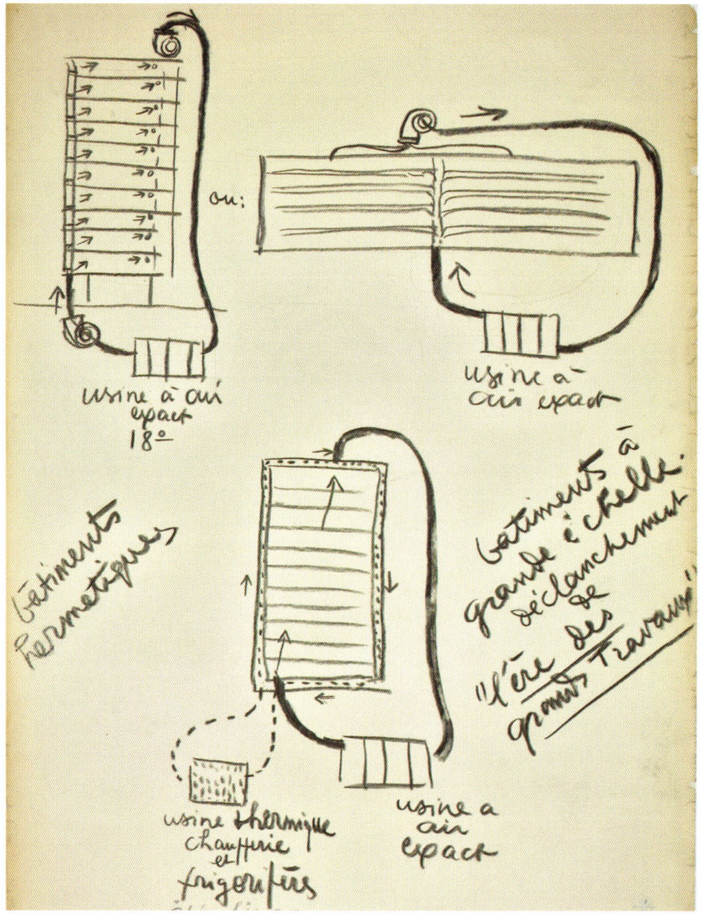

Salvation Army,
Le Corbusier, 1933

Our focus on environmental control was not new, but was built upon modernist experiments with building form and technology. Le Corbusier, for the Salvation Army, first imagined a smooth glass-faced object. To achieve it, he conceived the "neutralizing wall," or double glazing, and mechanical air conditioning. As it turned out, the project budget was insufficient to install air conditioning. After the building was occupied, the architect was called back to address inhabitant complaints of unpleasantly hot spaces behind the glass wall. This bioclimatic feedback loop caused him to reconsider the virtues of the modernist box with its taught glazed skin. He then reimagined the building with a thicker solar responsive façade. He saw this innovation as offering a new expressive kind of plasticity for buildings, which came to characterize much of his later work.

Our interest in effective solar design of façades similarly provoked an interest in the potential for plasticity and unique effects, as manifested in a number of projects, including the entry façade of a mausoleum.

In our firm, design assignments often turn into lines of cross-project inquiry. When invited to participate in the River Square design-build competition, we were interested in how a south-facing solar shade screen could be manipulated by inhabitants and syncopate the building facade facing a new public square. Our proposal was one of four done collectively by a team, including Kieran Timberlake, Gianonne Petricone Architects, and Waldman Architect. We based the typical residential suite concept on a prototype we had developed as a demonstration unit built for the Interior Design Show. We typically do not design condominium apartments, but this assignment gave us the opportunity to explore how they could be made to perform better environmentally.

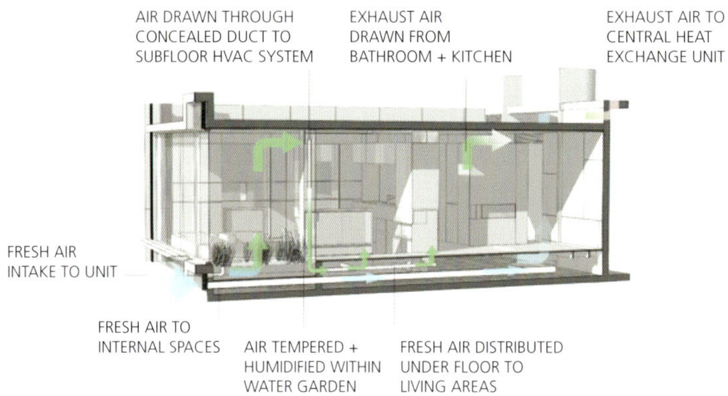

We imagined that we could deploy a raised floor system of the kind used in commercial offices so that all the services for the apartment would be within its envelope of ownership, not in the ceiling of the unit below. We realized that this raised floor could also serve as a ventilation plenum. By hooking it up to vertical air shafts at the interior corridor, similar to those used in Barcelona by Gaudi, we could create a stack effect system that would induce effective natural ventilation comparable to the through ventilation of a freestanding house with two exposed building faces. Another innovation for this project was the design of the north wall of the building to act as a sound buffer to the adjacent raised roadway of Eastern Avenue. A basket-weave facade provided acoustic defence to the north, while privileging views westward to downtown. We lost the competition and, regrettably, have never had an opportunity to implement this design.

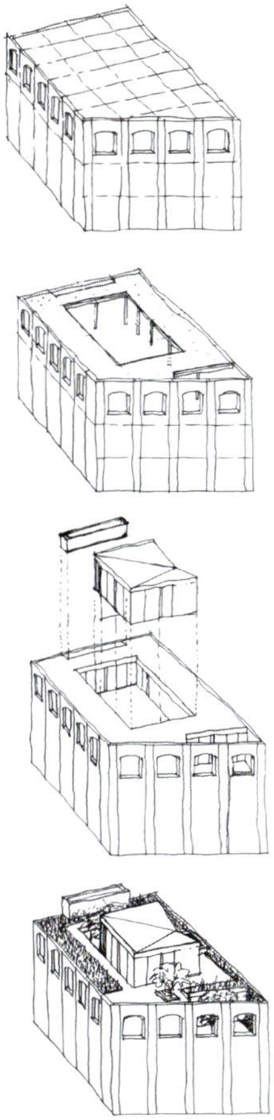

Although we could not find a developer interested in our condo tower concept, our client for the Ambrose Condominium warehouse conversion was intrigued by the raised floor idea. In this case, the challenge of the project was the large floor plate that resulted in poor daylighting and ventilation. We therefore deployed a dual strategy of subtraction to create daylight and ventilation courts in combination with the addition of raised floor areas where we needed them. The courts were paved for intensive use like the atrium of a classic Roman villa, while the roof was conceived as a wild garden in the cityscape.

How Does Architecture Give Form to Community?

The interest of the firm in civic action and civic space, developed in early urban design projects, continued to inform our approaches to building design as well as master planning and public space design projects. At the time of the millennium, we were engaged with a number of campus master planning studies in Canada and the US. The focus of these plans was typically twofold: to make better use of campus land resources through intensification and to improve the quality of community space amenities, most especially to improve student experience. On the University of Toronto's downtown campus, we were commissioned to do a study of the Devonshire Road area with the aims of increasing the supply of student housing and transforming the old Varsity Stadium site into a multiuse amenity, including a full array of athletic facilities.

The deployment of a residential building to create a new kind of campus community space also shaped the design of Erindale Hall at the University of Toronto Mississauga. Student rooms arranged in towers overlooking the landscape are interconnected by a raised linear bar building over a colonnade lined by glazed collective spaces. This colonnade provides cover and activity to a long cross-campus pathway that previously was insalubrious at night and in bad weather.

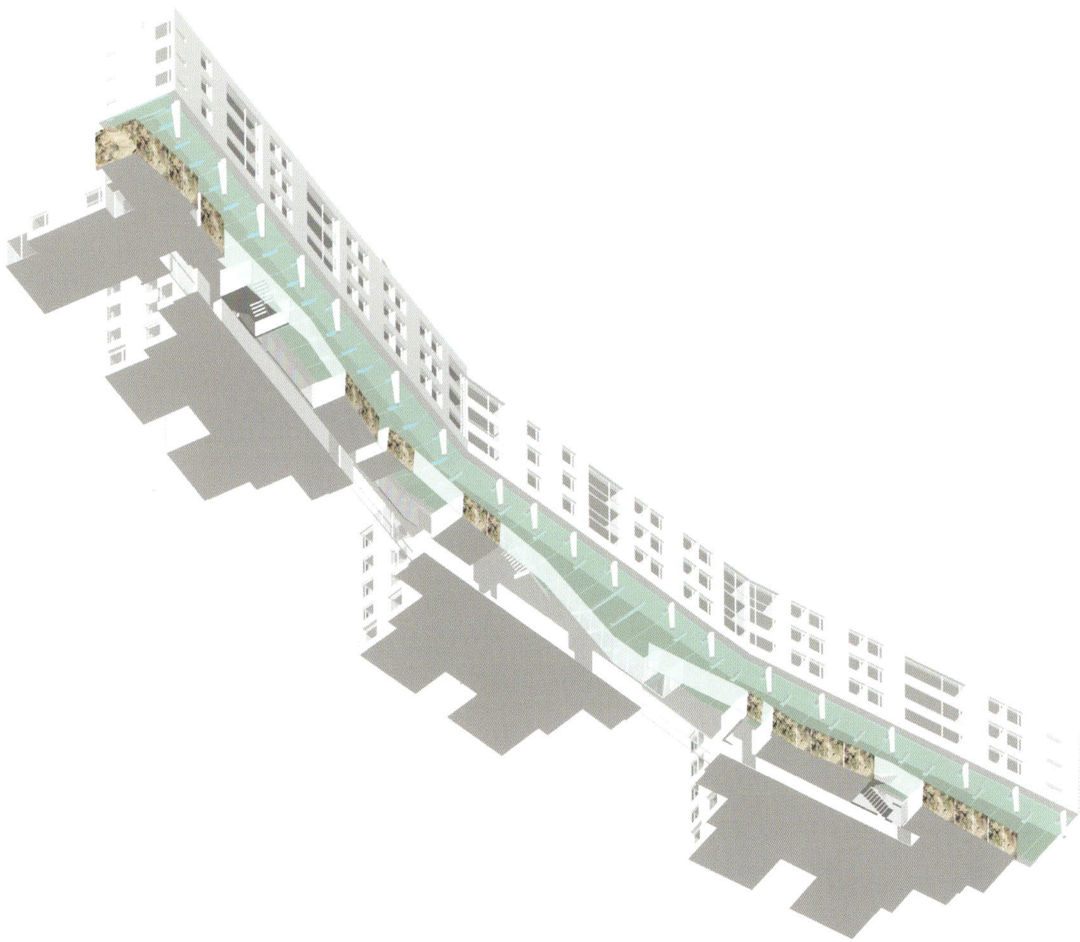

Over the years, many of my students at the University of Toronto have had to endure my reflections upon the writings of Walter Benjamin. In "The Work of Art in the Age of Mechanical Reproduction," he states:

> *Architecture has always represented the prototype of a work of art the reception of which is consummated by a collectivity in a state of distraction.... Architecture has never been idle. Its history is more ancient than that of any other art, and its claim to being a living force has significance in every attempt to comprehend the relationship of the masses to art. Buildings are appropriated in a twofold manner: by use and by perception – or rather, by touch and sight. Such appropriation cannot be understood in terms of the attentive concentration of a tourist before a famous building. On the tactile side there is no counterpart to contemplation on the optical side. Tactile appropriation is accomplished not so much by attention as by habit. As regards architecture, habit determines to a large extent even optical reception. The latter, too, occurs much less through rapt attention than by noticing the object in incidental fashion.*[7]

Appropriation of a building by touch and habit raises the importance of the haptic experience of architecture. At Erindale Hall, large water-pocked limestone cladding panels, evocative of the Credit River Valley on which the campus is located, alternate with super smooth undulating glazing. We discovered that capstone, from which the panels are made, is normally considered imperfect and thrown away.

A place for community sociability and events is also a matter of interior design. In the Roy Ivor Hall for the University of Toronto Mississauga, the entry hall is designed as a theatrical terrain for spontaneous or programmed meetings. A panoramic view of the exterior courtyard and pond reinforces the public character of the space.

The experience of weather outside and from the inside is a fundamental human condition and part of the haptic dimension of architecture. Experience of the weather as a community can bring us together in society. Similarly, coming together for ritual is a fundamental aspect of community. In the Prospect Cemetery Mausoleum, the glazed entry hall and stair provide a situation of quiet decorum for the arrival and entry of mourners into more private conditions of contemplation.

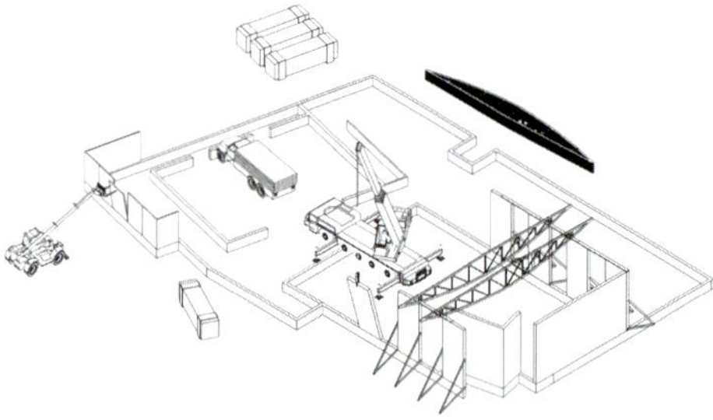

At Knox Presbyterian Church, just across the street from the University of Waterloo, our task as architects was to create a big, beautiful daylit room within an existing building where the church community could gather for its own rituals and social interaction. This room was also intended to be an attractive secular space open to the wider community to use for musical events and lectures. The key to realizing these community goals was to figure out a construction technique that would make it very inexpensive to build, and thus easier for the church community to manage financially. The small member trusses supporting the inverted arch ceiling are adapted from residential technology pushed to its limits.

The Cornell Botanic Gardens Visitor Centre is essentially a gateway to historic gardens, as well as a gathering space for visitors. It is, of course, designed to a high level of environmental performance, which includes a unique shading screen that creates a more unitary volumetric presentation to the building and defines a plane of passage. The centre is part of an integrated idea of promenade across the landscape, which begins with the parking and bus drop-off. A bridge over a new bioswale leads into the garden, and the swale planting adds a new ecological community to the garden's collection.

For our entry to the Nathan Philips Square competition in Toronto, we looked for subsidiary concepts in the Viljo Revell scheme that we could build upon to strengthen the original idea. Revell's design for the square included symbolic Canadian landscape references, including a copse of birch trees and the famous reflecting pond/skating rink – a notional northern forest and lake.

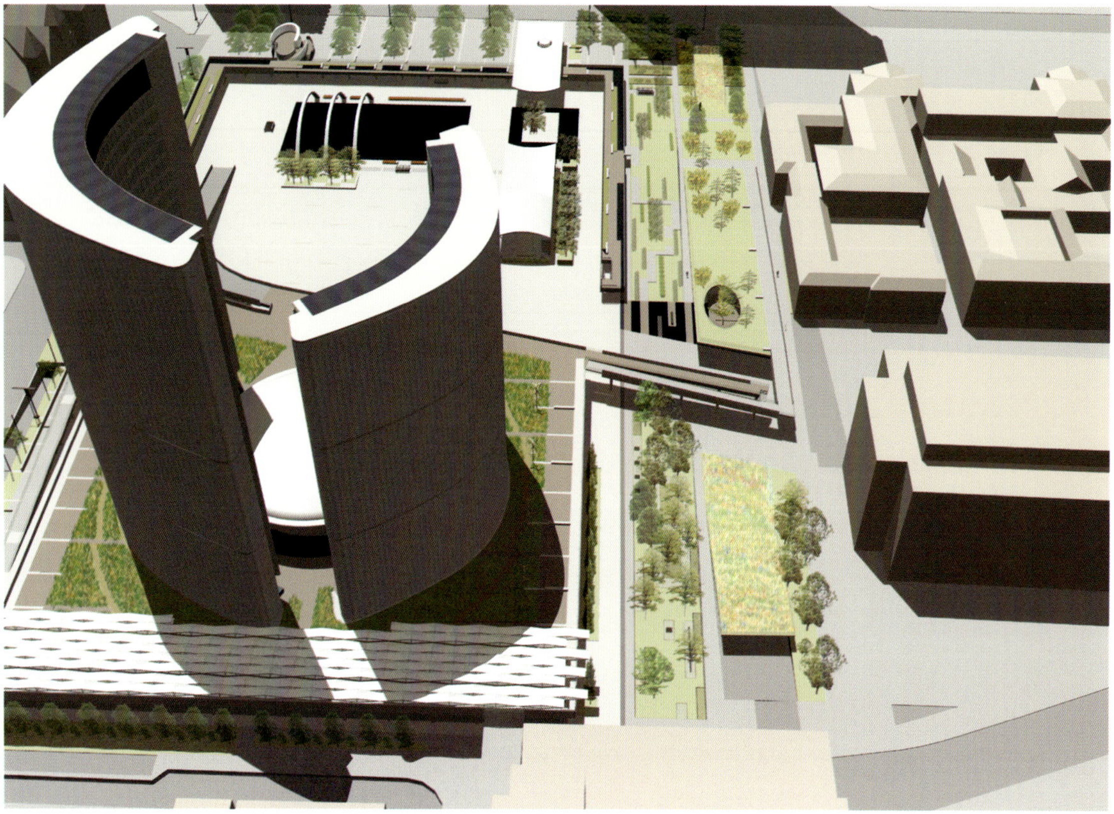

The theoretical context for our strategy was again provided by Walter Benjamin, and is explained in an essay titled "Reframing" that I wrote for the recently published monograph *boundary sequence illusion* on Ian MacDonald's work, in which I state:

> *In his book* The Origin of German Tragic Drama, *Walter Benjamin reflected on the meaning of the words "idea" and "concept," and made a clear distinction between "idea," denoting truth, and "concept," signalling intention. Benjamin argued that an idea is made up of a constellation of concepts, to which it gives meaningful order. Furthermore, he suggested the idea's essence is defined by concepts at the extremities of its meaning. For example, the Picasso readymade Bull's Head is made of the handlebars and seat from a bicycle. Bicycle is a readily understood idea, which is recognizable by essential constituent elements, each of which has an instrumental intention or concept. As long as these elements appear together in a certain order, regardless of their specific shape, the assembly is recognized as a bicycle. Picasso's sculpture shows how some of these concepts can be recombined to create other ideas. In this case, the specific form of each element is important: the handlebars have to be bent a certain way to evoke a bull's horns, and the seat shaped to evoke an animal's head.*[8]

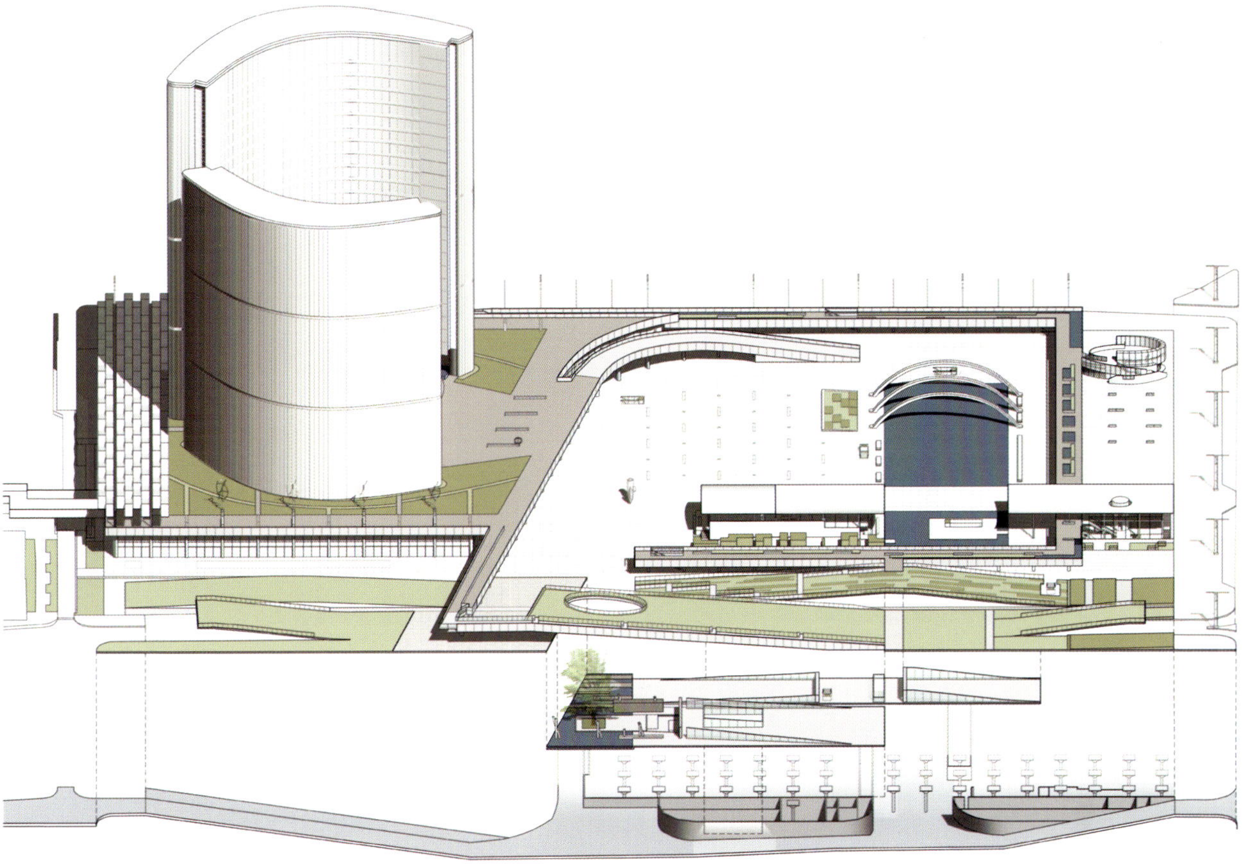

Benjamin's thinking also helped to shape Baird Sampson Neuert's proposal for Nathan Phillips Square. We pursued expansion of Revell's lake concept by making it longer and adding buildings bracketing the extension as rainwater receptors pouring water into the lake. This extended lake was designed with planting to clean the water. The proposal focused on making a tangible experience of being out in the weather. We similarly looked to expand the implicit topographical desire of the upper-level walkway by extending the promenade on the west side to make a complete loop. Then we warped the vestigial strip of planting on the west side to form a hill that would connect the upper walkway to the ground via a gracious landscape promenade. Below the hill, a glazed ramp was introduced to create an inviting daylit connection to the parking garage below the square. I regret losing this competition and the opportunity to expand Revell's constellation of concepts into a richer, more robust idea.

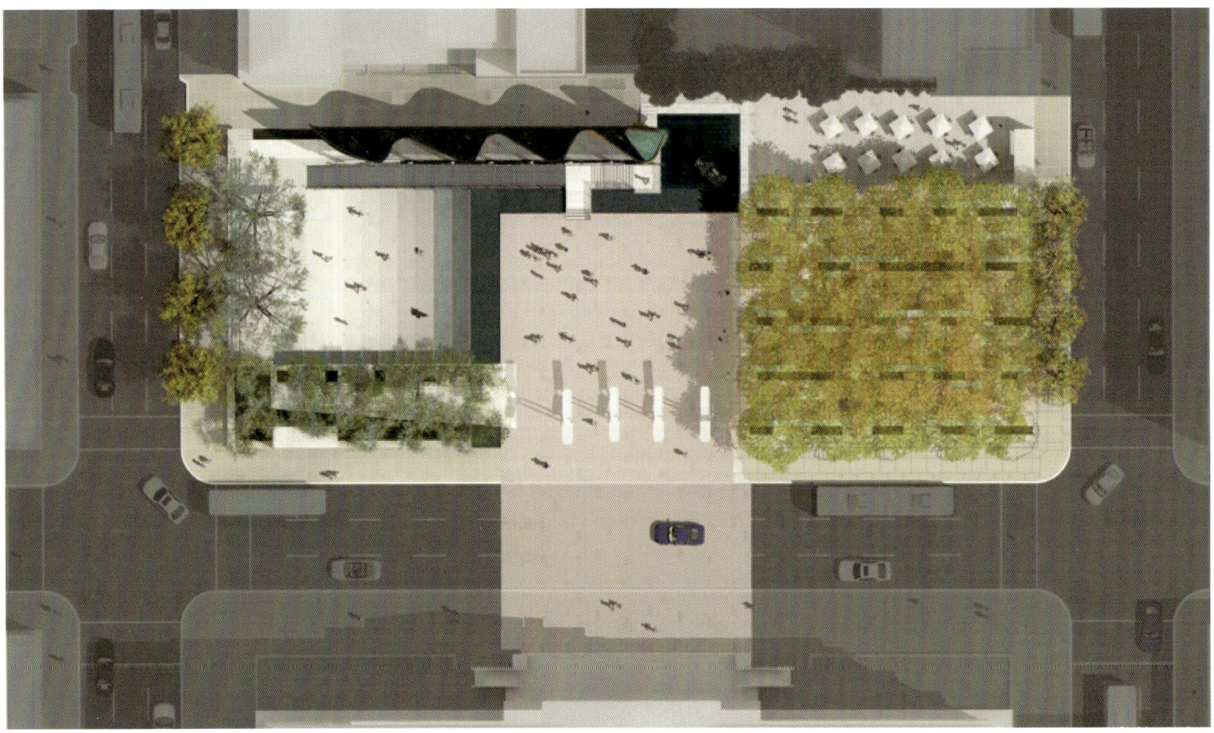

The Old Post Office Plaza in St. Louis was a project that we did win in a competition. Our design proposed a new space in the heart of the historic downtown that was intended to serve as a catalyst for its repopulation. The conversion, rather than demolition, of its many multistorey warehouses and commercial buildings into new condominium residences was the motivator for the civic leaders who sponsored the competition. The design idea developed as an architectural riff on the public art to be placed in the new plaza, a large bust called *Icarus*. For us, this brought into play the mythical history of Daedalus as the first architect of public space and evoked a narrative landscape. We designed a "cloud wall," an undulating zinc-clad surface on which ever-changing shadows of a perforated scrim would play. The continuous bench below the wall provides a shady spot to rest, and a ramped surface leads to a belvedere and waterfall, where the *Icarus* sculpture is displayed.

Can a Small Critical Practice Survive in an Age of Technocracy?

A few years ago, we worked on a design-build project with a development company in another city. Tragically, the head of the company died and the project was cancelled. Current public procurement protocols mean that it may have been our last opportunity to work on this kind of project. These protocols typically require demonstration of expertise through recent examples of the type of project being procured. This inherently favours larger firms that have a significant annual churn of work. The joke in our firm has been "We specialize in everything." We are attracted to technically challenging projects, projects that contribute to the quality of the public realm, and projects that enhance the quality of people's daily lives, such as university residences. We are architectural omnivores who do not design a lot of the same kinds of projects within a short time span.

We recently did not qualify for a university residence Request for Proposals because we had not done three buildings of the same use and scale in the last five years. In the same week, we did not qualify for an urban design master plan because we had not done at least three of the same type in the last ten years. The "procurement agents," or more impressively named "procurement officers," who are now in control of public sector architectural commissions seem to assume that principals in a firm either do not actively work on projects, or regularly forget everything they have learned on a five to ten-year cycle. For us, it is like being a young firm, with insufficient experience to qualify for a major commission, in perpetuity. We are not the only architects experiencing this technocratic prejudice.

A 2019 article in the *Irish Times* with the headline "Why are Irish world class architects not building in Ireland?" reinforces this point:

> *Grafton Architects have just won the 2020 Royal Gold Medal, but are ineligible to tender for many major projects at home.*
>
> *Their exhibition was internationally acclaimed, and yet… Grafton are ineligible to tender for many major projects in Ireland. This is because the procurement processes are so labyrinthine and strict that all but a handful of firms are excluded.*
>
> *Kathryn Meghen, chief executive the Royal Institute of the Architects of Ireland (RIAI), explains the situation [by describing] how public procurement policies are outlined at EU level, but individual countries interpret them differently. In Ireland, this is done stringently. For example, with a school project it is not unusual to have a stipulation that the selected architects must have designed between three and five schools in the immediately preceding years – begging the obvious question: if you're not allowed to design a school, how do get to design a school?*
>
> *Things are also often set up in such a way that only very large firms have the capacity to deal with all the paperwork. The result is that a tiny handful of large architectural practices scoop up the major projects, and in the process exclude, not only Grafton, but the exceptionally exciting younger practices in Ireland today.*[9]

Regardless of biases in the selection system, or our own failings, we have had to adapt. We are learning to look for the ledges, crevasses, and places out back that other firms may not have populated. Like Batman, we are up on the rooftops, working on non-traditional sites that do not touch the ground. At the University of Toronto Scarborough campus, we have been building out and restoring the original design intent of John Andrews's iconic building from the '60s.

In the Lassonde Mining Innovation Centre on the University of Toronto downtown campus, we have reclaimed an unused attic in the historic building for the installation of academic and meeting facilities, which include a new kind of collaborative space for creative engineering research and design modeled on the traditional architectural studio. Across King's College Road, on the top of the Wallburg Building, we are designing a new lab for engineering research into sustainable systems.

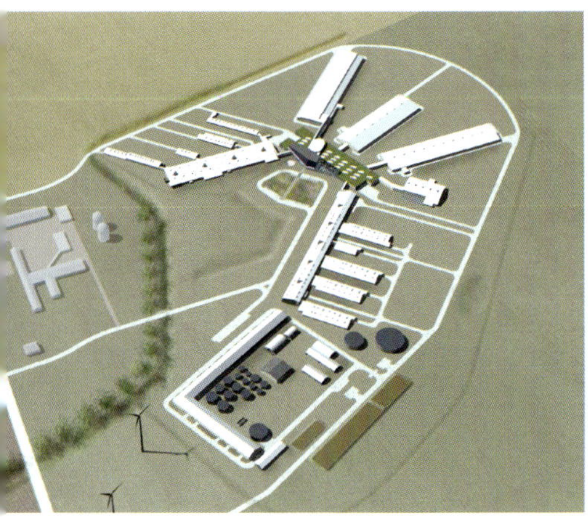

Our interest and expertise in bioclimatic design have also drawn us into the agriculture sector, where we are designing international leading-edge research facilities. We started a project called Mission 2050 by leading a diverse group of designers, climate engineers, and university researchers in the development of a new model for animal research facilities that could promote animal well-being, reform farming practices, and achieve net positive emissions, meaning all potential effluent would be converted to energy or products of value. By proposing to house different animal groups together like mixed farms of the past, Mission 2050 proved too radical for established agricultural industries. However, its research and environmental objectives continue to resonate in the agricultural sector.

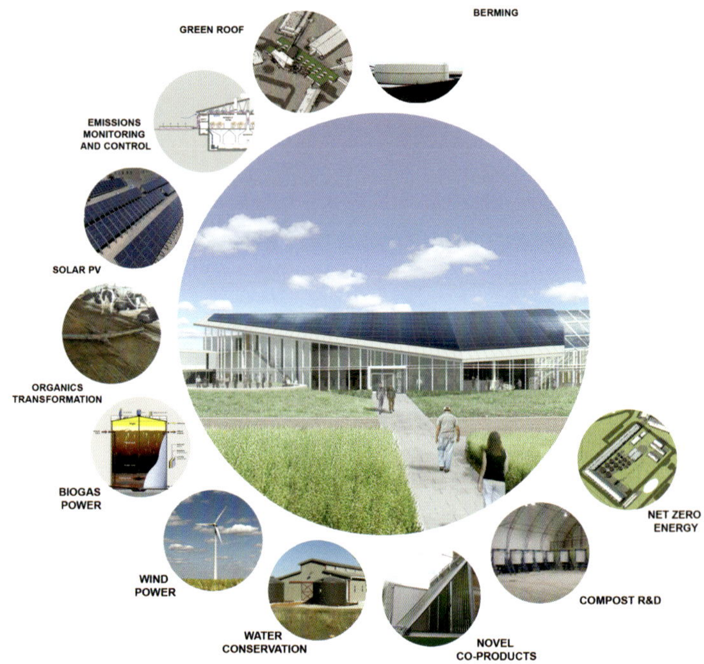

We recently completed the Elora Research Station at University of Guelph, one of the world's most advanced dairy research facilities, which includes the use of advanced robotics designed to enhance cow comfort and care. Also at Elora, we are designing a swine research facility that we hope will include an energy park first proposed in Mission 2050. In Alberta, we are working on a large agriculture centre that will focus on equine facilities.

These types of buildings are large in scale and require astute integration of animal support and environmental systems. We are discovering that they are more complicated to design than a university residence. At the opposite end of the scale spectrum, in the insect realm of agricultural research, we were invited to participate in the architect selection process for a Honey Bee Research Centre. Regrettably, we lost to Moriyama.

These kinds of commissions have deepened our understanding of our work on sophisticated greenhouse research facilities. In the Niagara region, we are master planning a major private sector funded centre for plant research. Our first building there combines highly controlled environmentally secure areas with other experimental production spaces that make use of computer-controlled weather responsive systems that we initially developed for earlier projects.

Another interesting suite of recent projects for our firm arises out of relatively mundane needs for visitor comfort and operational servicing. We are adding such a facility to the existing Allen Gardens complex, which will have a unique façade of stainless steel rods and glass. We have also been asked to explore the expansion of the complex into a into a world calibre botanical greenhouse, while making the site more conducive to community access and use.

Our experience with visitor centres like French River and Cornell Botanic Gardens has been pertinent to our work on Allen Gardens, and what we learned from their focus on site exposition and integration is also informing our approach to more ordinary service facilities on exceptional sites. For Humber Bay Park, we have been commissioned to install a visitor comfort and support station, as well as a separate service building. Taking a holistic approach to site research has generated a scheme that improves land and water systems, in terms of both ecological functions and user experience.

A major project that brings together many of our interests and skill sets is the McEwen Building for the Schulich School of Business at York University. For this project, focused on graduate study and research, our multifaceted interests proved to be advantageous due to the astuteness of the client. The fact that the project was a category-defying mixed-use building combining a residence with academic functions was an asset, as few other firms had repetitive experience of this kind of building.

The client asked for an idea – not a design – to be presented at the selection interview, to generate discussion with the selection committee. Using origami, we explored how a tower could be made into a signature element by a series of folds that would reorient the base building from the campus grid to an optimum solar south orientation for climate responsive design. Unfortunately, a change in University policy led to cancellation of the residential tower.

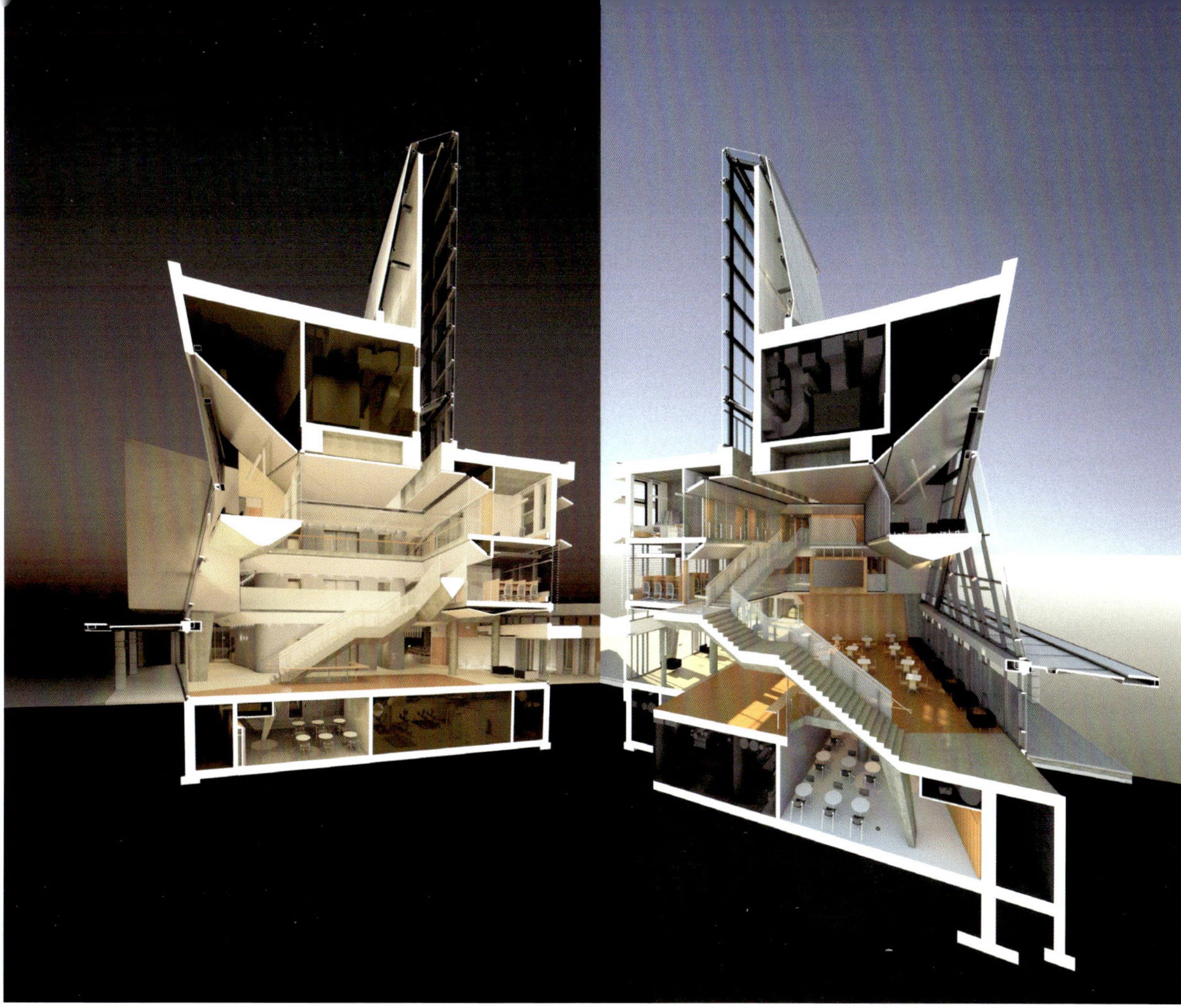

However, exploration of how we could integrate an effective solar chimney to boost weather responsive, stack-driven natural ventilation remained of interest to the client. The solar chimney was therefore retained as a central part of the hybrid mechanical and weather responsive environmental control system for the building. The chimney is situated above the central atrium, which stretches from the street to the court. The atrium is designed to be a place of sociability and idea exchange, as well as the hub of air exchange for the natural and mechanical ventilation system. In this way, integrated multivalent functionality creates opportunities for new form.

A sculptural stair wraps the atrium, creating a theatrical edge that connects the main activity space at grade to a bridge lounge on the third floor. The faceting of the original origami idea presented to the selection committee is reprised in the unique plastic form of the stair and lounge structure.

The structure of the stair extends through an opening in the atrium floor to provide visual connection and daylight to a basement lounge and locker area. Blackwell Engineering, our structural design partners, worked creatively to integrate our architectonic strategy with the building's structure. More importantly, we used our knowledge of integrated environmental systems design to create a user environment focused on well-being as well as community. When we go to the building, users often spontaneously tell us how much they enjoy being in it and how well they feel compared to being in other buildings on campus.

The design success of the McEwen Building and many of these projects makes me optimistic about the future of Baird Sampson Neuert architects. I hope the exploration of questions of practice I have considered here provides a sense of why I believe the firm has a strong and unique voice in Canadian architecture.

I have also pursued some of the themes I have discussed through the design of several experimental houses. The Mackowiak Residence is a concrete dwelling that investigates the interplay of solar light and energy with heavy plastic mass. The house is covered with meadow grasses to integrate the new structure into the site's ecology. It is designed to open to the sun and shelter from the clouds.

In another project, a hand-built cabin from the 1950s has been lifted and wrapped with a high-performance envelope to save it from a trip to the landfill – a fate that is befalling many seasonal cottages of the era across Canada. Posing an alternative to demolition, this approach reuses and transforms a piece of the cultural landscape into a multigenerational gathering place and an all-season oasis. The themes of compactness and adaptability, first demonstrated to me in Rietveld's Schroeder House, are here very much in design play.

La roche est escarpée, l'eau est profonde je suis au desespoir. Pag.
LA NOUVELLE
HÉLOÏSE
TOME I.er

Epilogue

On a more personal note, I am no longer a young man with years of patience ahead to grapple with the current environment of technocratic risk management that makes the economic environment for firms like ours challenging. I love both teaching and practice, but decided to simplify my messy work life by retiring from teaching, as well as stepping back from practice to a degree. Jon Neuert, aided by our very capable staff, is now ably leading the firm forward. He has been dedicated to achieving the highest quality of design, environmental performance, and project delivery since he joined the firm.

Having thought long and hard about the meaning of retirement and having started this lecture with a reference to Rousseau, I will close by returning to his writing. For me, this is also a return to the beginnings of my teaching career, just after doing research in France into the relationship of urban innovation in Paris and developments in French landscape traditions, from the classical garden to the picturesque. The latter caused me to read *La Nouvelle Heloise* by Rousseau, and made me curious about his other writings. His summation of retirement is found in the last chapter of *The Reveries of the Solitary Walker:*

> *The idleness I like is not that of a do-nothing who stands there arms folded totally inactive and thinks no more than he acts. Mine is both the idleness of a child who is in perpetual movement, but does nothing, and that of a dotard who combs the countryside while his arms are at rest. I love to busy myself with nothings, begin a hundred things and complete none, go and come as the spirit moves me, change projects every moment, follow a fly in all its buzzing around, try to uproot a rock to see what is underneath, undertake a ten-year task with ardor and let it drop ten minutes later without regret, in sum, to muse all day long without order or coherence and follow in everything only the caprice of the moment.*[10]

For those who are into the hurly-burly of professional life, this must sound somewhat attractive. For a person of my age and decrepitude, it is a siren call. However, I still have some work to do and will leave chasing the flies for a little later.

Practice

George Baird

Barry Sampson was born in 1948 in Oshawa, Ontario, and spent his childhood and youth there, arriving at the University of Toronto in 1967 to commence his education in architecture. He and his classmates arrived just as a dramatic new curriculum was launched by Peter Prangnell, under the aegis of the newly appointed chair of Architecture, John Andrews.

I first met Barry the following year when I joined the University of Toronto as a new faculty member. He was never directly my student, but we knew each other at a distance. Then, upon graduation in 1972, Barry – together with his classmates Joost Bakker, Bruce Kuwabara, and John van Nostrand – came to me and proposed that they join my fledgling one-person architectural practice. I was taken aback at this proposal, but we found a way to make it work – at least for a period of time. After a few years, Joost, Bruce, and John left the practice for various reasons. Barry stayed, and we worked together for the next 30 years.

In the early years of our professional relationship, Barry served as a valued backup to me in my role as principal designer at the firm. Key projects of that early period, in which he played an essential role, include the Dunbarton-Fairport United Church in Pickering, Ontario, and the "Ontario's Main Streets" study we undertook for the Ontario Heritage Foundation. It was already apparent that his dedicated commitment to execute projects so that tectonic details were consistent with the original design ideas was an invaluable asset to the firm. Then, in the late 1970s, he took a sabbatical from the firm and went to work in Paris for a year on the understanding that, upon his return to Toronto, he would become my professional partner.

When he returned, the second stage of our long professional relationship commenced. On our 1982 entry to the Edmonton City Hall competition, and the 1983 Trinity Square Park competition, he continued to play the invaluable backup role to my lead. But with our successful – finally! – entry to the 1990 Bay Adelaide Park competition, our roles shifted. This project was a design collaboration between the two of us, and it launched a period during which we worked together on projects including the Butterfly Conservatory for the Niagara Parks Commission, and the housing project on Maybank Avenue in Toronto for the Supportive Housing Coalition. Some years later, we rejoined design forces for our winning entry in the design competition for Old Post Office Square in St. Louis, Missouri.

Later still, the volume of work of the office expanded to such a degree that we began to divide projects – initially between Barry and me, and subsequently, when Jon Neuert became our new partner, among the three of us. While I focused primarily on a series of mausolea and columbaria for the Mount Pleasant Group of cemeteries, Barry and Jon took design responsibility for several much-admired university residence buildings at the University of Toronto Mississauga, as well as at the Scarborough campus. Finally, when my academic responsibilities became too demanding, I retired from the practice altogether, and Barry and Jon took it over entirely. During this period, Barry was responsible for a number of major projects, including the Thomas L. Wells Public School and the new building for Knox Presbyterian Church in Waterloo. Probably the building from this period of his career of which he was proudest is the McEwen Building for the Schulich School of Business at York University, a project with one of the highest environmental ambitions of any in Canada. Throughout all the years of his activity at Baird Sampson Neuert, his commitment to develop projects that remained true to the original design idea never flagged.

In addition to his important role at Baird Sampson Neuert, Barry also came to play an important role in architectural education in Canada. To the best of my recollection, he first joined the academic faculty at the University of Toronto as one of a cadre of younger designers who I invited to teach during my brief chairmanship in the mid-1980s. Since we were professional collaborators in practice, we agreed that we would not teach together at the university. As a result, it is only after his death that I have come to learn the depth of admiration for him as a teacher from his colleagues in Toronto and elsewhere, who did teach with him over the years. Despite his initial reluctance, he discovered that he was a highly effective pedagogue, ending his academic career as one of the most admired teachers in the entire recent history of architecture at the University of Toronto, as well as across Canada.

Thomas L. Wells PS
ELEMENTARY

Thomas L. Wells Public School, 2005

Thomas L. Wells Public School was commissioned by the Toronto District School Board as a model of sustainable design and place for high-performance learning. It became the first elementary school in Canada to receive a silver rating from the Canadian Green Building Council's LEED program, and was recognized with an American Institute of Architects Honor Award in 2008. The design of the school is exemplary for the ways it fosters social interaction among children in the school, and between the school and the surrounding neighbourhood. It is a model for the integration of public institutions, civic space, and bioclimatic design. The LEED certification acknowledged the building's significantly reduced operating energy and maintenance costs, and the high quality of interior spaces with enhanced natural ventilation, ample daylighting, and indoor/outdoor connections. A follow-up study in 2011 confirmed energy performance, which significantly exceeded expectations, and acknowledged the building's role in promoting student achievement and major improvements in assessment scoring in reading, writing, and math.[1]

Located in Morningside Heights, a suburban subdivision at the eastern edge of Scarborough, the school serves a multicultural community in which the majority of students speak a language other than English at home. As the only public building in the development, the elementary school is designed to be the focus of civic life in the neighbourhood. The H-shaped plan establishes a centralized community hub that includes the school's library, gymnasium, and principal's office at its core. An internal circulation spine extends through the hub, linking the sheltered entry forecourt along Nightstar Road to the school's playing fields and Birunthan Park, and to courtyards within the school.

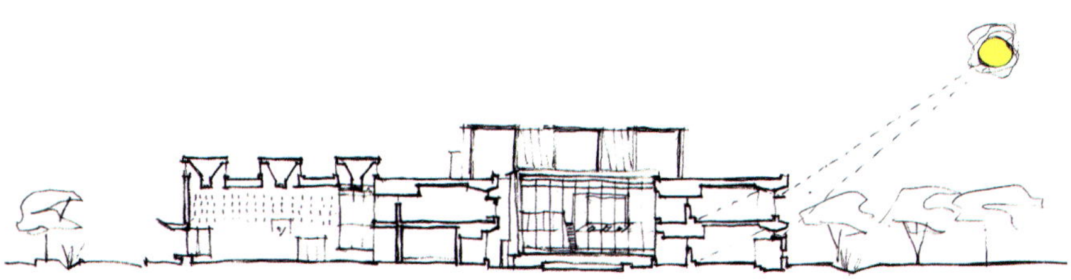

1 gymnasium
2 stage
3 service court
4 staff lounge
5 administration
6 offices
7 kindergarten
8 classrooms
9 library
10 music
11 science + technology
12 art
13 computer science
14 rooftop garden

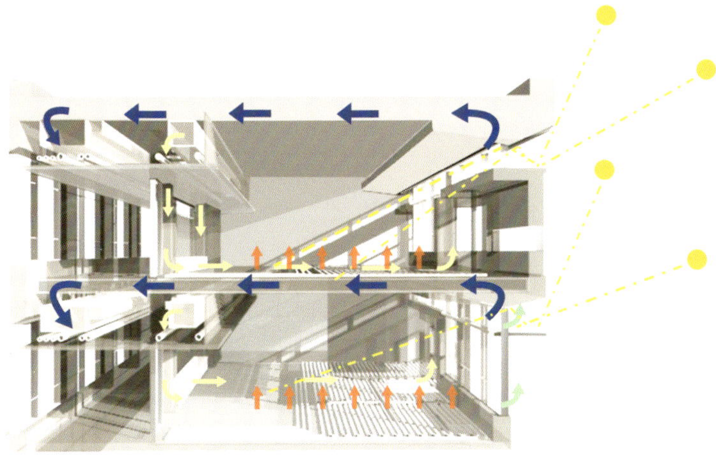

Section through classrooms

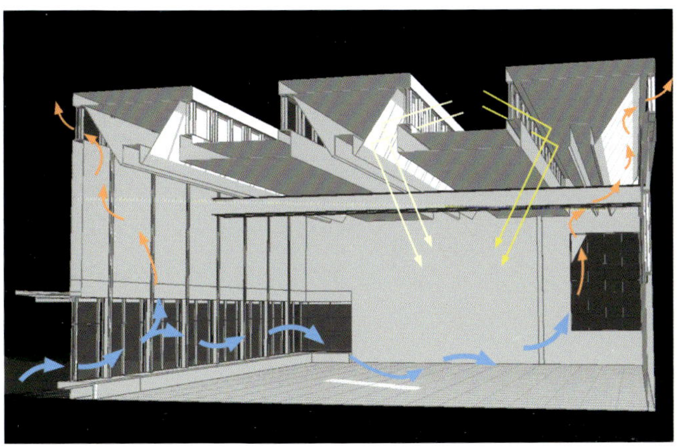

Section through gymnasium

Immediately adjacent to the entry forecourt, the gymnasium is a multipurpose community space for assemblies, performances, sports, and public events. Visually connected to the street by a fully glazed façade, its transparency promotes community engagement with interior programming and events. The double height library – the academic and social focus of the school – is positioned at the intersection of the four classroom wings, which frame outdoor courtyards used for teaching and recreation.

The school's massing and integrated "system of systems" are designed to enable high human and environmental achievement. The H-shaped plan of the building is oriented to optimize daylighting conditions for classrooms. The building's northern wing is double loaded, with the forecourt, administration and gymnasium facing north to the street, and classrooms facing south. In the southern wings, classrooms are accessed along single-loaded glazed corridors that overlook the courtyards. The classrooms have ample glazing for both views and daylight. External and internal light shelves, which were analyzed using radiance studies, shade windows from summer heat gain and reflect low winter sun deep into the plan. High- and low-level operable windows promote natural chimney ventilation to reduce reliance upon mechanical cooling, while providing age-appropriate interior sill heights.

The building's precast concrete floor and masonry structure provide thermal mass to harvest winter solar energy and retard summer heat build-up, and are an integral part of the unique displacement air ventilation and radiant floor heating system that utilizes the cores of the precast slab as part of the ducting system. The gymnasium has operable roof monitors, which extend the length of the space to provide controlled indirect daylighting and exhaust hot air using standard greenhouse operating equipment. Demonstration solar panels supply a proportion of the school's energy requirements. Durable materials reduce maintenance and promote long-term sustainability.

This integrated systems approach improves the energy performance of the building while enhancing comfort. The use of daylighting, in combination with radiant floor heating and natural and displacement ventilation systems reduces reliance on noisy mechanical equipment, creating a bright, comfortable, and quiet learning environment. At the same time, the organization of plan and section promotes social interactions and visual connections. Views extend from the classrooms to courtyards, playing fields, and the park beyond. While the corridors offer views into the courtyards and library. The special education classroom – a sculptural volume projecting as a "treehouse" in the library – is located at the heart of the school.

Intended to guide new school construction in the Greater Toronto region, Thomas L. Wells Public School subsequently received awards from the Ministry of Energy, Ontario Conservation Action Team, the City of Toronto, and *Canadian Architect* – awards that recognize the importance of integrating environmental metrics of sustainability with strategies to promote human achievement and develop social infrastructure for newly established communities.

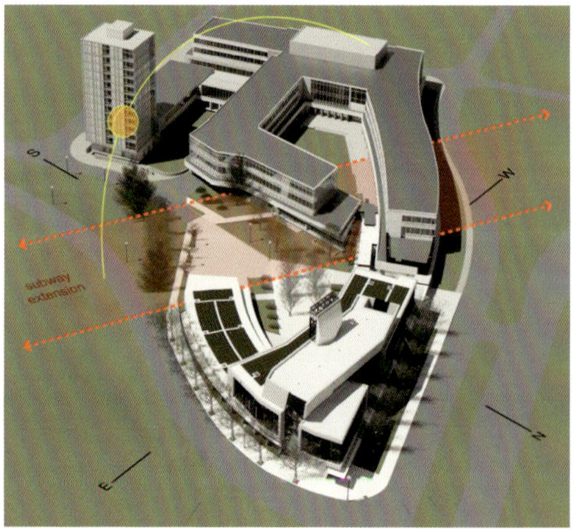
S
W
subway
extension
N
E

Penthouse
1 mechanical
2 electrical
3 solar chimney
4 green roof

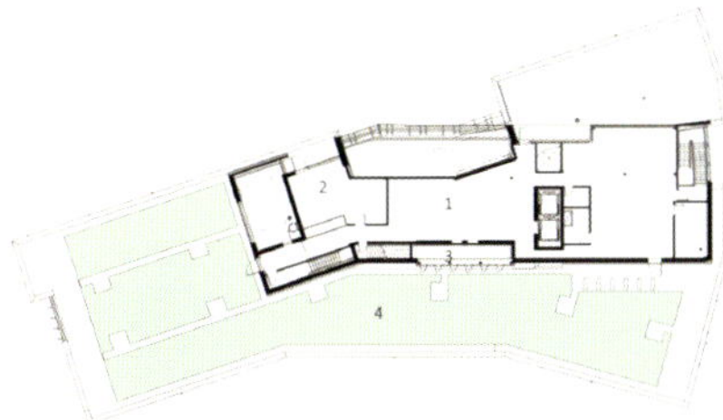

Second Floor
1 atrium / social hub
2 graduate lounge
3 seminar room
4 staff office
5 study carrels
6 reception
7 research lab
8 research office

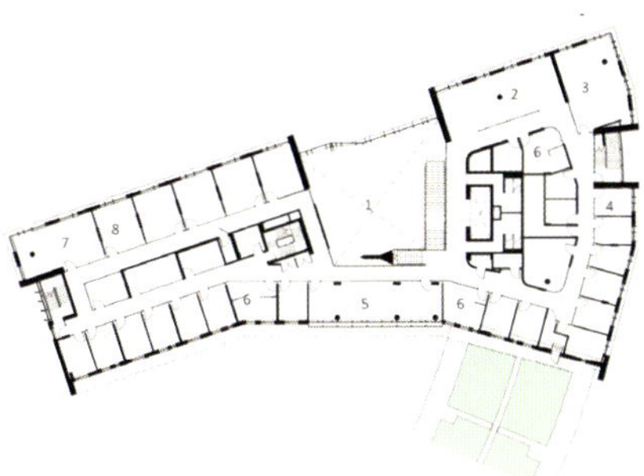

Ground Floor
1 main entry
2 social hub
3 teaching spaces
4 seminar rooms
5 breakout rooms
6 café

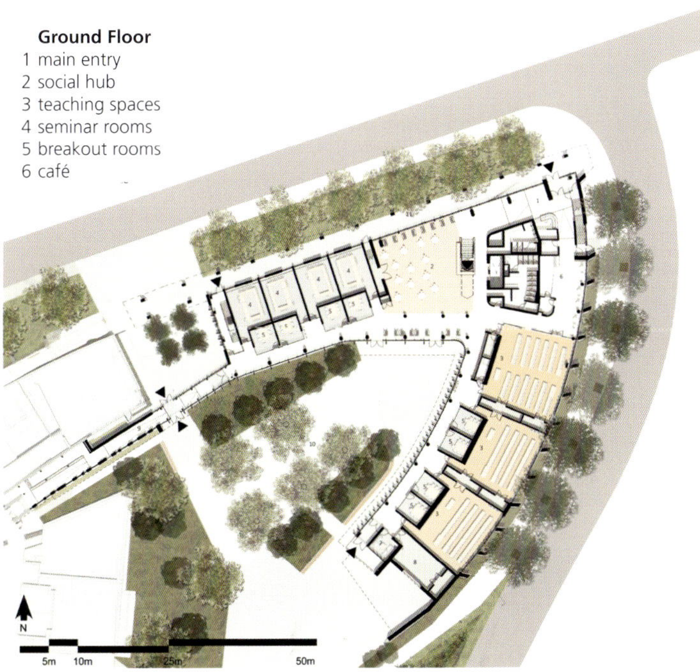

Rob and Cheryl McEwen Graduate Study & Research Building, 2019

The McEwen Building, an expansion of the Schulich School of Business at York University, combines an environment for collaborative research and learning with exemplary levels of environmental performance that reinforce the school's global leadership position in sustainable business education. Situated at the eastern gateway to the campus, the unique form of the building is the result of the synthesis of climate responsive design, a focus on the well-being of occupants, and the response to a challenging urban context which included coordination with subway construction under the site. The three-storey building wraps the perimeter of the site to create a south-facing courtyard, which extends the existing system of courtyards that characterizes the School. Entrances from the courtyard and the street converge in a central atrium which is the performative hub of the building's social and environmental systems. The atrium connects with a solar chimney that drives the building's bioclimatic design approach. A significant new campus landmark, the solar chimney projects the centrality of sustainability in the school's educational curriculum.

The building is designed to enable different pedagogical approaches and learning styles that create opportunities for collaboration. At ground level, a flexible array of large classrooms, seminar rooms, and breakout spaces opens into an atrium café. These facilities can be selectively programmed or used in combination to support a variety of workshops, conferences, teaching modes, informal meetings, and special events. On the second and third floors, offices and research labs are clustered to foster collaboration and mentoring between faculty and students. The clusters are organized around the perimeter of the building by a loop corridor, with core and support facilities in an inner band.

The atrium is crossed by horizontal and vertical pathways on all levels, establishing routes that foster spontaneous social interaction and promote collegiality. A sculpted concrete stair that rises through the atrium leads to a quiet lounge on the second floor, and an open bridge lounge on the third floor. Overlooking the social hub and street, the bridge lounge can also be used for events and digital conferencing.

A hybrid passive/active ventilation strategy is intertwined with this network of spaces to create a "building that breathes." Massing and orientation optimize daylighting, shading control, passive ventilation, and energy harvesting opportunities. The south-facing solar chimney, located above the social hub, extends almost 30 metres above the atrium floor. Solar heat collected within the chimney induces passive ventilation throughout the building when hot air is released via high level automated vents. This system adapts robust greenhouse ventilation concepts and applies them systematically to realize an ultra-low-energy environmental system. Windows, sized to address specific ventilating needs of individual spaces, are modulated by an automation system that operates in concert with the solar chimney using real time information from the building's weather station. Manual override is available for every window, using controls with signal lights to guide occupant use. During the winter heating season, hot air collected in the chimney is used to preheat incoming air, enabling increased levels of ventilation without energy penalty. The absence of large fans and the extensive use of acoustically-lined air transfer ducts provide an interior environment that is remarkably quiet.

The building's high-performance envelope features thermally-isolated construction throughout, and a 40 percent window-to-wall ratio. All spaces have strong visual connections to the exterior. To ensure effective daylighting in occupied spaces, the distribution of windows was informed by iterative daylight and shading studies. High performance triple-glazed insulated units with spectrally selective glazing are calibrated to optimize visible light transmission and solar heat gain, according to orientation. Detailed thermal modeling of glazing systems, including mullion divisions and operable windows, ensured the mechanical design accurately reflected whole system glazing performance values throughout. Canopies, shade awnings, louvred screens, and vertical fins are located relative to seasonal sun angles and sized to mitigate solar gain overload of the low-energy cooling system. Clerestory glazing is strategically unshaded and uses light-diffusing frosted glass to maximize daylighting effectiveness.

The project's sustainability strategy prioritizes environmental conditions that promote user well-being, through low-energy/high-performance design. The project has a projected ultra-low energy use of 72.4 kWh/sqm per annum, and provides 83 percent energy and 68 percent carbon reductions. A net-zero energy study outlined renewable energy technologies and pathways for the client to incrementally realize net-zero objectives. The building's seamless integration of urban, social, educational, and environmental strategies has been recognized with major awards, including the CaGBC Ontario Green Building Award and, in 2020, the Canadian Green Building Award and the Ontario Association of Architects Award of Excellence.

Integrated social and climate responsive design

1 solar chimney rack and pinion awnings for preheat intake and natural ventilation exhaust

2 solar chimney rack and pinion skylight damper

3 solar chimney mass wall with intake dampers to Dedicated Outside Air System (DOAS)

4 mechanical penthouse with DOAS

5 radiant acoustical ceiling panels and baffles

6 active slab radiant heating and cooling

7 curtain wall and triple glazed fibreglass windows with automated operable vents

8 solar shading to south elevation

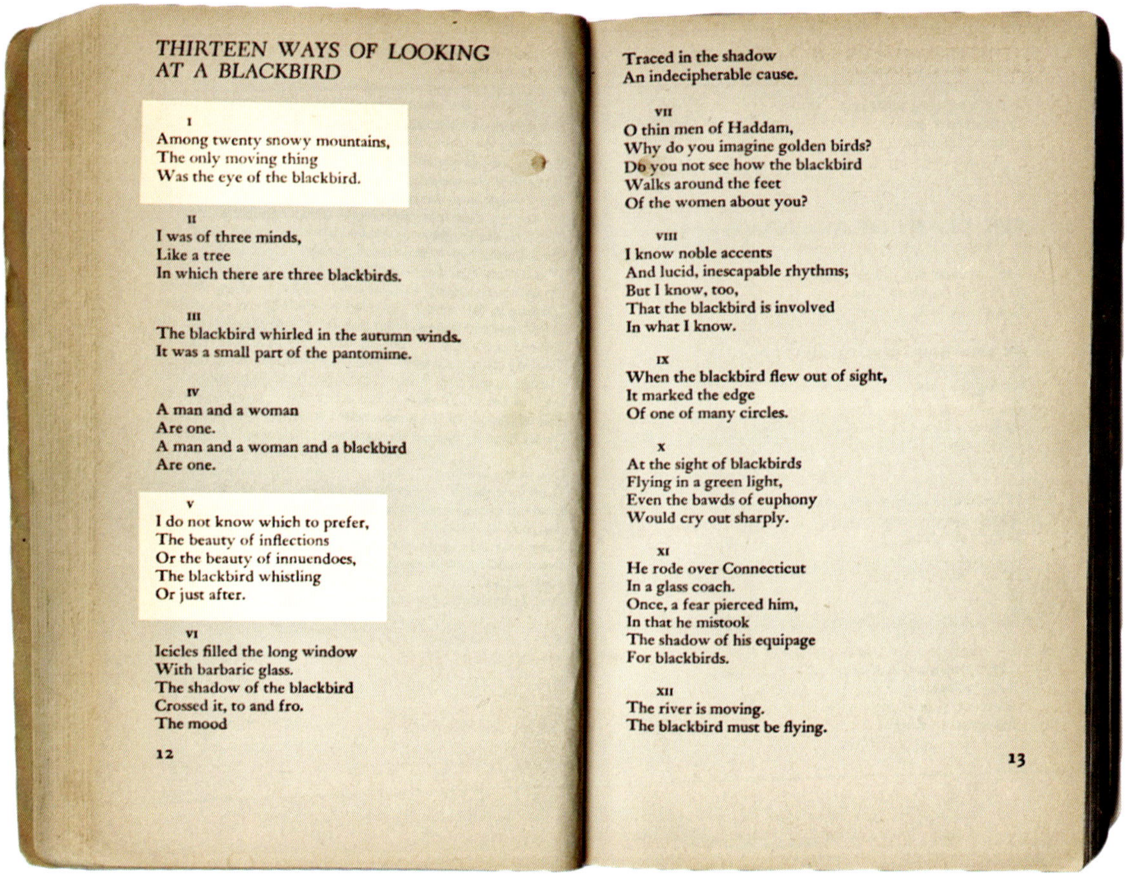
THIRTEEN WAYS OF LOOKING AT A BLACKBIRD

I

Among twenty snowy mountains,
The only moving thing
Was the eye of the blackbird.

II

I was of three minds,
Like a tree
In which there are three blackbirds.

III

The blackbird whirled in the autumn winds.
It was a small part of the pantomime.

IV

A man and a woman
Are one.
A man and a woman and a blackbird
Are one.

V

I do not know which to prefer,
The beauty of inflections
Or the beauty of innuendoes,
The blackbird whistling
Or just after.

VI

Icicles filled the long window
With barbaric glass.
The shadow of the blackbird
Crossed it, to and fro.
The mood

12

Traced in the shadow
An indecipherable cause.

VII

O thin men of Haddam,
Why do you imagine golden birds?
Do you not see how the blackbird
Walks around the feet
Of the women about you?

VIII

I know noble accents
And lucid, inescapable rhythms;
But I know, too,
That the blackbird is involved
In what I know.

IX

When the blackbird flew out of sight,
It marked the edge
Of one of many circles.

X

At the sight of blackbirds
Flying in a green light,
Even the bawds of euphony
Would cry out sharply.

XI

He rode over Connecticut
In a glass coach.
Once, a fear pierced him,
In that he mistook
The shadow of his equipage
For blackbirds.

XII

The river is moving.
The blackbird must be flying.

13

Jon Neuert — Cultivating an Integrated Terrain – Lessons, Recollections, and Genealogy

The collected poems of Wallace Stevens – Barry's favorite poet – were sitting on his bedside table at his cottage at the time of his death. The highlighted passages from Stevens' "Thirteen Ways of Looking at a Blackbird" served as introductions to talks and lectures Barry delivered and, in many respects, represent his embodied mode of thinking as teacher/architect and mentor/artist.

Situated in an immersive landscape, the watchful "I" of the blackbird is both part of and separate from its environment. When set in motion through space and time, sensations, fragments, and varied perspectives give rise to limitless possibilities. Barry's interest in phenomenology – a sensory and experiential architecture – stimulated a lifelong exploration and quest for an integrated and expansive idea of holistic design. The uncompromising aspect of the blackbird and the demand for excellence were poured into his students, his work, and especially me.

I recently came across a fragmentary set of speaking notes for a lecture Barry delivered on the firm, dating from 2003, that had the working title "New Terrains." His notes outlined our "unusual partnership" and encapsulated his perception of the synergies and intergenerational contributions to the firm:

George Baird: *architecture and the space of appearance – politics/urbanism/architecture*
Barry Sampson: *architecture – an analogous landscape*
Jon Neuert: *architecture and the question of sustainability*

The "terrain" concept, manifested and synthesized through his teaching and the collaborative oeuvre of the firm, embodied Barry's deep interest in phenomenology, providing a broad platform to develop, test, and actualize a pedagogical approach focused on integrated design. It also served as a means to synthesize the contributions of three generations and define a terrain of practice.

A Terrain for Mentoring and Teaching

My initial interactions with Barry occurred as a first-year student during the tumultuous year of 1984 at the University of Toronto's School of Architecture and Landscape. As studio coordinator, Barry developed a highly innovative and fully integrated studio program for 48 architecture and 24 landscape students, which shared common projects and instructors from both departments. The studio experience was reinforced by a theory and history course for the combined class, also taught by Barry. Lectures incorporated his personal research into French gardens – Sceaux, Vaux-le-Vicomte, Buttes Chaumont, and others – conducted during his 1979 Paris sojourn, when he studied at the Sorbonne and worked with Devillers/Cheomotov. Asplund's Skogskyrkogården, Le Corbusier's architecture promenade, and Aalto's haptic naturalism were synthesized through the phenomenology of corporal experience, movement, and memory.

While the term "integrated terrain" was not yet part of the educational lexicon, the concept of architecture as an analogous landscape was a foundational idea for experiencing, understanding, and informing design. A take away of our analogous landscape education was the recognition that human activity was not inherently external to natural systems, as encapsulated by the wonderfully simple teachable concept that humans and other species build, rearrange, and modify the environment – implanting an idea of nature as cultural construct.

Terrains of Experience

Early public space projects developed collaboratively with George Baird and others – including Regina Traces, Trinity Park competition, and Cloud Gardens – advance a space of appearance, improvisation, and social agency across a constructed landscape of interconnected indoor/outdoor spaces and experientially diverse kinesthetic terrain. The reoccurrence of the glasshouse – a set piece of garden design, and Walter Benjamin's reading of modernity's roots in the iron and glass construction of 19th century Parisian arcades[1] – was a central thematic element of an integrated and itinerant experience of place, and activated four-season use. The infusion of nature within the city, and the historical patterns of the landscape as a responsive idea to site and placemaking, are perhaps best expressed by our multiple attempts to reassert Taddle Creek in Toronto.

In 1990 I was invited to join the practice as an intern, and was immediately immersed in the design development of Cloud Gardens, working under Barry's direction. The demands of the conservatory served as a technical grounding and immersion into the first principles of bioclimatic design. This exploration of bioclimatic design expanded the dimensions of a socially-activated and analogous terrain of experience, becoming part of the constellation of interests that shaped the firm's understanding of design excellence.

Terrains for Future Exploration

Barry's leadership role in the development of the University of Toronto's comprehensive building studio provided a testing ground and accelerator to explore new terrains of integrated design. The growing imperative of climate change, and need for broad action, fostered a belief that architects had the requisite technical skills as designers and integrators of the built environment and, therefore, the moral imperative to provide professional leadership in confronting this existential crisis of our time.

While committed to design conceptualization, Barry bemoaned facile applications of the "signs" of sustainability, and advanced a synergistic process of inquiry to understand the means and measures necessary to deliver tangible outcomes, using first principles of bioclimatic design supported by rigorous testing, modeling, and analysis.

This ethos permeated Barry's teaching and our shared design outlook and practice. This new terrain activates possibilities for innovation on par with the breakthroughs that accompanied the onset of modernity – innovation that is desperately needed to address the pressing challenges of our time and respond to the demands of a new epoch.

Refusing to blend in, or become anything less than it is, the blackbird takes flight in new form, still whistling, or just after.

Teaching + Practice

Robert Wright

Brigitte Shim

Ian MacDonald

Pina Petricone

Erik Olsen

David Bowick

In Conversation:

Richard Sommer

& Nader Tehrani

Robert Wright

I met Barry in the early 1980s when we were both sessional lecturers at the Faculty. I had just come to Toronto to teach part-time after ten years in professional practice. The Faculty had been in a state of turmoil for many years, and had won a hard-fought battle over the University's proposal to close it. In many ways, it was a very fragmented working environment, of which I was blissfully unaware. Barry took me under his wing.

Barry and I shared an interest in French gardens, which we discovered when I commented on his firm's 1983 Trinity Square competition entry, which I admired then and still do. I mentioned that its uses of topography reminded me of Jean-Charles Adolphe Alphand's design for Parc des Buttes Chaumont, which had been constructed in an old quarry. I still remember the light in his eyes as the ever-present sketch book came out. After that, our conversations around landscape architecture expanded, deepened, and evolved.

Barry loved the book *Gardens of Illusion: the Genius of André Le Nostre* by Franklin Hamilton Hazlehurst.[1] He was fascinated by Le Nostre's use of surprise and illusion, created through subtle changes in landform, planting, and perspective that directed views and manipulated spatial perception. This influence, I believe, is subtly evident in all of Barry's site work.

In 1989 I became a full-time member of the Faculty, and our landscape conversations continued for over 35 years, broadening to include English picturesque, Italian, and Japanese gardens. In addition to historical precedents, we discussed contemporary work influencing landscape architecture, including the 1982 Parc de La Villette competition and the 1999 Downsview Park competition. Barry constantly challenged me to think about design more synthetically, as a continuum in which the design of building and site is fully integrated.

As a true modernist, Barry was always eager to demonstrate in his sketch book how the work of Le Corbusier, Alvar Aalto, Louis I. Kahn, Carlo Scarpa, and others could be translated into landscape. At the same time, he was fascinated by how landscape architecture could more fully explore and express its knowledge of natural environments, climate, geology, ecology, horticulture, and garden history. He had a particular passion for how the Canadian landscape could be interpreted in both ecological and formal terms. I believe that both Trinity Square Park and the Bay Adelaide Park Cloud Gardens are good examples of Barry and his firm's formal exploration and integration of program, circulation, planting, and topography.

Barry mentored me in my transition from practitioner to academic, and in the relationship of design and construction. He lamented that many academics separated that relationship in design instruction. To Barry, they were inextricably bound together. He showed me the intersection and true potentials of design relationships in landscape and architecture that transcended professional boundaries. His impact was not only on me; it echoed through the Faculty and the many students he taught.

As Associate Dean under Dean Larry Richards, I participated in the Faculty's annual graduation ceremony at Convocation Hall. In those days it was a long, drawn-out affair, which included hooding of each student and longer conversations with both the Provost and President of the University. Robert Prichard was the University of Toronto's president at the time, and he would ask questions of each student as he offered his congratulations. When the students of the Faculty of Architecture, Landscape, and Design came forward to receive their degrees, he asked: "Who was your best teacher? From whom did you learn the most?" Standing next to the President, ready to shake each student's hand, I would hear repeatedly "Barry Sampson, Barry Sampson, Barry Sampson," until it became almost a mantra. On one occasion after several years of this, President Prichard turned to me and said, "This Barry guy must be one great teacher." He was and still is.

Brigitte Shim

I knew Barry Sampson as a student and graduate, as a fellow architect, and as an educator. As a valued friend for almost four decades, he enriched my life. In the early 1980s Barry was a frequent visitor to reviews of student work at the architecture school at the University of Waterloo, invited by our professor, Donald McKay. I respected his ability to provide deep insights into the varied student projects pinned up for discussion. It was clear that he was someone who knew a great deal about the worlds of architecture, landscape, and urbanism, who could quickly analyze each project from many vantage points, and provide surgically accurate comments that enabled students to see their work with clarity.

After our final thesis reviews, Barry invited my classmates Jon Soules, Howard Sutcliffe, and me to assist with a competition entry that Baird Sampson Architects was preparing for Trinity Square Park. We immersed ourselves in their picturesque landscape proposition. While not premiated, this project was important for the firm, and was the precursor to their winning entry for the Bay Adelaide Park competition, which was built some years later.

I worked at Baird Sampson Architects for the next five years. During this time Barry was a valued mentor, who generously shared his passion for the work of Carlo Scarpa, André Le Nostre, Gerrit Rietveld, James Stirling, and many others. While working on projects in the office, it was apparent that Barry derived great pleasure from the complex act of putting buildings together. His joy was most palpable when he was able to spend time at his drafting board. When he was really happy he would sing while drawing.

My partner Howard Sutcliffe and I were starting to design and build our own projects, mainly furniture, and Barry made time to give us in-depth reviews of a chair and other small projects. In these informal critiques, he always talked with us, not as students or recent graduates, but as colleagues. He conveyed his love of the architectural promenade as well as his keen understanding of the crucial role that drawing plays as a critical tool for thinking and designing. He fundamentally believed that small projects were important vehicles for exploring architectural ideas. We experienced first-hand Barry's approach to integrated design thinking – the benefits of fusing architectural ideas with building technologies and structure.

Time spent with Barry as a faculty colleague in the chaotic studio spaces of 230 College Street, reviewing student work and discussing ideas about architecture, further deepened my own architectural education. He possessed a set of remarkable skills that enabled him to guide generations of students through initial research and many subsequent stages of design development, always drawing out the best work from each individual. It was fitting that he developed the pedagogy for the comprehensive building studio at the school, as it was an accurate reflection of the way he conceptualized buildings that he was designing.

Barry's own cottage on Beech Lake was a living prototype that enabled him to experiment and test many of his ideas. Howard and I spent several years building our own living laboratory on an island in Georgian Bay. During Barry's last visit to our Harrison Island camp, the Canadian landscape provided a fitting backdrop to our ongoing conversations about life and architecture.

Ian MacDonald

Barry Sampson was a fearless, talented, and socially responsible architect and a profoundly influential teacher, and it was my great good fortune that he and I became close friends.

I was somewhat nervous about meeting him for the first time, knowing of his academic and professional prowess, but I found out quickly that he was also very real, almost ordinary in his way with people. I got to know him well when we taught first-year studio together at the University of Toronto from 1984 to 1999. Barry developed the curriculum and constantly refined it over time. That first-year program became recognized as central to the school's identity.

After final reviews in one of the early years of the program, we were all quite thrilled with what the students had managed to achieve. The teaching team – sans Barry – was assembled in our small office on the third floor of 230 College Street. We were sharing our collective observations about the quality of the student projects, practically high-fiving each other in celebration, when we heard Barry's distinctive footfall as he approached. Everyone adored and respected Barry, and was looking forward to the pleasure he would hopefully have found in the work. When he entered the office as we were preparing to discuss marks, he exclaimed in a huff, "We blew it!" He went on to add, "If the scale of the required detailed section drawing had been 1:20 instead of 1:50, the students would really have learned something." This critique took the wind out of everyone's sails, but the following year that change was made and, sure enough, the results were much improved. It was Barry's extraordinary ability to focus on the key concepts being taught, and to constantly revise elements of the studio curriculum, that would lead to a stronger program. In this regard, in my view, he had no equal.

His high level of consciousness about the making and experience of architecture allowed him to engage with any student no matter how obstinate, provoking, or confrontational, and to turn every exchange into a teachable moment. He was up-to-date on cultural reference points for the younger generation and, including these in his critiques, often helped build bridges of understanding that would otherwise have been lacking. Barry was an inspired bridge builder. This consciousness was the result of his wide-ranging interest in how things worked, from social groupings to the physics of environmental concepts, and from guitars to poetry. His naturally inquisitive approach to just about everything gave him a wide reach and access to most people and situations.

Barry contributed an essay to *boundary sequence illusion: Ian MacDonald Architect,* the monograph on the work of our office that was published in 2019.[1] In this essay, he set out a context for the framing of an idea in art, architecture, photography, and painting, explaining clearly how the way in which a work is framed is central to its meaning. He referred to the work of various artists and identified that central to them all was "the search for essential characteristics and conditions of environment within particular sites that are resonant with the human experience and imagination.... [I]n this sense artists focused on reframing sites and situations in pursuit of an idea." He added comments on the use of types, the hearth, exaggerated transparency, and sequence, recognizing that our projects could not be experienced in a single view frame but only "through a process of apperception activated by moving through the space." Having been in practice for over 40 years, this clear explanation of the work we had done is something I could never have articulated. Barry was exceptional in his ability to do this and, on top of it all, he possessed a wonderful, self-deprecating sense of humour.

Pina Petricone

Never one without the other, Barry Sampson taught and practiced for over 40 years. His ethos in each discipline depended on the simultaneity of thinking, speculating, and doing. Although I did not have the privilege of being his student, Barry introduced me to practice and taught me about teaching.

After graduating from the University of Toronto, I joined Baird Sampson Architects as an intern in 1991 and, leaving for graduate school two years later, I had learned lessons from Barry that still guide me in my work. Drawings are constructions that are affected by a form of gravity through their inherent layers, so the foundation of a drawing should be omnipresent even if receding under heavy lines of a section. After all, the generative aspect of a section is unparalleled, and a plan is simply a horizontal section. For Barry, a model – like a landscape, a building, or a city – is inventive when it builds in complex dynamism that evolves through time and in context.

This kind of dynamism is subtle but potent, and it might be the enduring constant that allowed Barry to shift seamlessly between theory, teaching, and practice. I would describe it as a kind of performance that Barry demanded from his work and the work of his students, and where I believe Barry found joy in the capacity for architecture to make a positive impact on the world.

After joining University of Toronto's Faculty of Architecture in 1995, I sought out every opportunity to teach with Barry, and managed to do so at just about every level of the professional program. Some 20 years later, I had the privilege of taking over Barry's comprehensive building studio after he retired, and I continue to strive to do it justice. As founding architect of our comprehensive building studio, Barry led the University of Toronto in the promotion of integrated design as a sophisticated, ambidextrous, and creative exercise. His approach to sustainable practices in architecture and urban design as inseparable from seminal design strategies, rather than as inventories of must-have "features," was central to his teaching innovation. As colleagues, we all witnessed how far this strategy went in introducing students to the reaches of design, and in dispelling the notion that conceptual rigour is limited to the initial stages of formal investigation. He lived by this approach in practice, and it is recognizable in his most exemplary and accomplished projects.

In January 2018, I invited Barry to present his recently completed McEwen Building to the comprehensive building studio as an example of integrated design from concept to completion. In one short hour, we were invited into his nimble, sophisticated, and inspiring process of thinking, speculating, and doing.

Supported by sketch models, sectional models, photographs, drawings, sketches, section perspectives, and diagrams, Barry tailored the presentation to students. He invited us all to witness the complexity of practice as something to be celebrated in design, not as something to resist or be frustrated by. He lingered on the seductive concept model that, with a few pieces of precisely placed white card, expressed all the ideas for the project – conceptual to technical. He methodically took us through those ideas as well as touching on the external forces that ultimately shaped the project, including the University's decision to eliminate the housing tower. As an audience, we mourned the loss of the residential volume that surrounded and perhaps financially justified the solar chimney. However, Barry slowly but surely revealed the resulting building's tectonic logic, which depended on – among many other elements – the solar chimney as a key element of the scheme, not only for its literal performance but also for its performance as a social condenser of the future campus.

Barry opened this presentation by declaring that comprehensive building design "is what architects do," assuming the definition of architect as master builder. This definition, embodied by Barry, views the act of building as a form of teaching and learning. To build requires intellectual, conceptual, and moral rigour that must seek out and integrate a wide range of expertise, as well as respond to external forces.

Our search as architects is never-ending and makes us all students forever. Barry's success and immeasurable impact on the formation of students and spaces alike was a result of his full understanding of this critical aspect of practice and teaching.

Erik Olsen

I am acutely aware that I knew Barry for a much briefer period than many of his professional and academic colleagues, and am honored to share some thoughts based on our short experience working together. I first met Barry as we began collaborating with Jon Neuert and the BSN team on the Mission 2050 project in 2009, and our relationship deepened as we worked more closely on the McEwen Building for the Schulich School of Business.

What was immediately apparent was Barry's thirst for life-long learning. This accomplished architect and teacher, 30 years my senior, was deeply engaged in every conversation we had and committed to expanding his knowledge in pursuit of truly high-performance human-centered spaces. Understanding the reasoning behind the design choices we recommended was critical to him. I have found few collaborators who seek to internalize ideas from other disciplines so thoroughly. This deep understanding equipped him to steward an ambitious idea through the inevitable ups and downs to a successful built project that we hope serves as an example to others.

I was also surprised to discover how Barry's curiosity extended beyond the boundaries of a project. The last time I saw him was at the 2019 RAIC Festival of Architecture, where we did a joint presentation on the McEwen Building. He had come well-prepared to spend our time together digging into the latest questions on his mind. After our presentation session, he thoroughly quizzed me on the interaction of radiant systems and thermal mass. Somehow, I do not think our conversation slaked his thirst for understanding the topic.

Barry's deeply caring nature was manifested as very patient persistence when necessary. When he served as a Faculty advocate for One Spadina, the new Daniels building, he recruited me to provide additional technical support. I watched from the sidelines as he tirelessly worked to help the project meet his own high standards. He mercifully spared me from most of the many difficult conversations that are necessary in such an advocate role.

I now fully appreciate that my experience with Barry was not unique. John van Nostrand speaks of Barry as an architecture student, thriving with the juxtaposition of theory and intuition promoted by different faculty. My recent interactions with First Nations architects in Canada have introduced me to the dual contributions of western reductionist thinking and Indigenous ways of knowing, which I cannot yet claim to fully grasp. Now I am the one thirsting for a chance to discuss this dualism with Barry, as I suspect it would be obvious to him. It is how he approached his work for 50 years.

Barry used his inquisitive mind to effectively show us how simple and elegant low-impact architecture can be. He always challenged himself to go farther. Our cross-generational exchange, so unusual in architecture, reflected his open mind and spirit.

David Bowick

Barry Sampson taught me many things and inspired me in many ways. He taught me about the importance of architecture and its impact. He taught me about humility, and he taught me about craft.

I met Barry when I was working for Yolles as the structural engineer on the Niagara Parks Butterfly Conservatory. It was not a huge project for Yolles at that time, which was accustomed to massive developments with the likes of Olympia & York, but it was treated as an important project and became pivotal for me in my development as an engineer.

Barry loved structure and wanted to express it. The building was unique in form and geometrically complex. The structure needed to be integrated with the form of the building. Up to that point, I had not recognized structural design as part of the creative process, but rather imagined the engineer's role as being simply to make the architect's ideas stand. Working closely together, he challenged me to think beyond precedent.

He also made me aware of the extraordinary knowledge base an architect must have to create architecture. I watched Barry and his partner, Jon, become experts on butterflies to design the conservatory and, subsequently, experts on dairy cows after being appointed to design the Guelph Research Dairy. They learned about Canada's Indigenous peoples while designing the French River Visitor Centre and, at the same time, they were becoming experts in all the disciplines under the design team umbrella. This enabled them to continually challenge consultants to do better, particularly in thinking about sustainable design and passive building systems.

Barry enjoyed concrete for its beauty, its permanence, and its thermal mass. Many of the projects we completed together celebrated concrete and pushed its use as an architectural element. Together we designed a gravity-defying cantilevered concrete stair for the Old Post Office Plaza in St. Louis, and the even more ambitious sculptural concrete stair at the Schulich School of Business at York University. The beautiful board-formed concrete walls at the French River Visitor Centre were designed to incorporate cast-in crack-inducing sonotubes to generate small well-distributed cracks rather than the usual required control joints. The extraordinary curving walls of the Mackowiak House incorporated a bespoke thermal break that we developed specifically for that project. We designed precast light shelves for the Thomas L. Wells Public School. There was always a new idea, a new challenge – myriad beautiful columns, walls, floors, fireplaces, and other architectural details.

By no means limited in his aspiration, Barry's structural ideas also allowed us to hone our craft in the structural design of wood. Knox Presbyterian Church explored the use of low-cost prefabricated light wood trusses and wall panels to create a substantial sculptural building. The French River Visitor Centre incorporated large moment-resisting glulam frames and floor-to-roof wall trusses to achieve a dramatic cantilevered tube of exhibition space. The McMichael Gallery incorporated some of the first cross-laminated timber in Ontario. The Humber Bay Park Pavilion will be a voided concrete-timber composite, a unique hybrid of mass timber and concrete with plastic ball voids.

There is little Barry would not try. He did wonderful things with glass in projects like the Butterfly Conservatory and the Discovery Landing in Burlington, which needed slender expressed steel structures. For the ceiling of the OCADU Gallery, he explored the design of tensile fabric membranes.

Barry frequently invited me to be a guest in his comprehensive building studio at the University of Toronto. He would ask me to prepare a primer lecture for his students to start their thinking about structure for their projects. No problem to solve, just blue-sky thinking. It was enormously challenging to distill all of structural engineering into a one-hour lecture. It inevitably became a lecture on a philosophy of structural engineering, and Barry always appeared to appreciate it.

He would occasionally ask me to participate in a game of "stump the expert." This involved him showing images of structures from a survey of modern architecture and challenging me to explain the structure and identify the load path. I was a young structural engineer, and he was a brilliant architect at the peak of his career, but he called me the expert. Through these survey lectures, he introduced me to the beauty of Aalto, the importance of Le Corbusier, and the influence of the Bauhaus. I am grateful for the perspective this has given me.

In Conversation:
Richard Sommer & Nader Tehrani

Richard Sommer: Nader, can you remember your first encounters with Barry?

Nader Tehrani: We met through George Baird and at reviews in Toronto over the years, but my first real engagement with him was on the competition selection panel for the Daniels Faculty Building, which was the original renovation project for 230 College Street.

RS: Barry was very much at the centre of that process, writing the program and setting a high bar for environmental performance. Of the five shortlisted firms – Steven Holl, REX, Sauerbruch Hutton, Behnisch Architekten, and Office dA – my read was that your submission was not among those he favored. You were not at the top of my list either, but for different reasons than Barry's.

NT: If I remember correctly, you were enthusiastic about Sauerbruch Hutton, because the project was supposed to be about reskinning the building. They had done interesting cladding-based projects and this would have been their first building in North America.

RS: Yes, but the scheme your office presented and the thinking it represented completely swayed the competition jury. In the final voting, you won by a significant majority. However, I am not sure Barry was fully convinced. I had just arrived as the school's dean and, in my discussions with him, he questioned your "baroque" sensibility. While everyone liked the idea of choosing an up-and-coming architect, Barry asked me whether I thought you – and at the time, Monica Ponce de Leon – were going to be the real thing or a flash-in-the-pan. We had some work to do to engage him in the project.

NT: Then you did what seemed like this crazy thing of abandoning the renovation, which was not even funded yet, and going after a project more than twice the size at One Spadina. We undertook many studies on the new site because of its urbanistic implications, its need to engage with larger community groups, and its environmental impact at large. There were even schemes, some including residential towers as a funding mechanism, which took us all into another universe far from the original competition.

RS: Barry was upset by my abandoning 230 College, which he had carefully upgraded over many years, because he felt we were finally close to finding a way to significantly improve the building. He was not the only one to think that my pursuing a more ambitious project at One Spadina was folly, and that we could not pull it off, but he was one of the few who was frank with me about it. I think he was a bit angry with me; around the same time, he told me he intended to retire from the faculty. I tried to stall his decision. On many important issues facing the Daniels Faculty, Barry was sometimes the only real adult in the room who had survived the school's troubled past. I felt that his expertise was critical and that having his support for the construction of a new building would be key to bringing many of our colleagues on board with the idea.

NT: I was not aware of this background. There was a faculty committee that advised us and, after the initial studies, when the strategy was endorsed by the University and became a real project, Barry became your main advisor and therefore also our main advocate. From the start, Barry brought forward questions and ideas that were different in kind than our focus: how to best model and test the program; how to address Provincial and University building standards that are not set up for flexible, studio-based environments; and especially how to bake environmentally sound logics into the project with regard to energy, lighting, air quality, and acoustics.

RS: Once I convinced Barry that the project was going to happen, I got him involved in helping us figure out the architecture and systems at every scale. Barry loved architecture. More importantly in this case, given my limited experience in Toronto and the University of Toronto context, Barry loved the process of making architecture – the fight, if you will. With his title as Special Advisor, he came to wear many hats.

NT: For us, he started out as a critic and coach. Then he evolved into a collaborator who was deeply invested in the relationship between design features and their corollary technical performance. At one point, when we were far along in developing the scheme, he was dissatisfied with the approach we had accepted from the local consultants – rightfully so, I should say. He convinced us to have Erik Olsen of Transsolar lead a peer review for the project. This made us nervous, especially my then-partner Katie Faulkner. Transsolar recommended several changes, including using a bubble deck for the main plate of the new building to lighten the structure and to allow most of the servicing systems to be integrated into the slab, with radiant heating being a critical component.

RS: The University of Toronto's capital projects people were dismayed by this move, sensing cost and schedule implications, but Barry and I both knew and trusted Transsolar. All along, Barry had argued that our project should be a model of innovation in every way possible. I started out thinking that Barry was, by sensibility, conservative (though not politically) and risk-averse, but I would not have gone forward with what were risky changes if he had not pushed them, with the understanding that he would have my back. We ended up building one of the few bubble decks of this kind in Canada. By the end, our roles had in some ways flipped: I became a bit weary of the process and, like you, fretted over every compromise and aspects of the project that were not as well-executed as we wanted. Barry became more buoyant over time and was our best advocate. When he and I did regular walk-throughs toward the end of the contract, he would remind me of how much we had accomplished and say how the project "is amazing and something to be very proud of."

NT: Barry always prevailed through patience and a slow-cooking method. He forced us to study things down to their details – their means and methods, if you will – and to examine their implications within the larger arc of the project. He was invested in a wholly integrative process and was generally dissatisfied with random gizmos that might be specified for the building. The signature piece of One Spadina, the vaults over the studio space – an essential element given the depth of the plan – were almost value-engineered out. Originally conceived as concrete, as an extension of the floors below, they were to be cast overhead. Seeing warning signs from the contractors of impending costs and a complex construction process, Barry was determined to have us develop a way to see this element through without compromise.

Ironically, it was precisely his astute understanding of compromise that allowed the vaults to be saved. He had us investigate alternative ways of constructing them to optimize the weight and method of construction. The shift to steel trusses in tandem with the gypsum board ceiling panels radically simplified the delivery and reduced the cost of the roof. In this one gesture, the structural, daylighting, and hydrological aspects of the roof were woven into a single assembly, something the project could not have achieved if it were not for Barry's stubborn persistence.

It was perhaps the biggest battle of the project, but after the revised roof was finally approved, Barry would look at me with a subtle smile, acknowledging an achievement that was not so much architectural but procedural and political in nature. He had great skill and character as a clinically rigorous and highly principled professional. At the same time, he was deeply empathetic and humble on a personal level. It was this combination of qualities that helped us realize One Spadina for the Daniels Faculty and Toronto.

Four Tributes: Barry Sampson, 1948–2020

Canadian Architect
December 20, 2020

Bruce Kuwabara

Donald McKay

John van Nostrand

Joost Bakker

Bruce Kuwabara

Barry Sampson, the architect

From 1967 – the year I met Barry as a first-year architecture student at the University of Toronto – to the last conversation I had with him in November 2020, he was the same person: deeply thoughtful, gently humorous, friendly, and courageous. His family has lost a loving partner and a father, while the world of design and education has lost a remarkable, ethical and creative architect, and teacher.

As an architect of distinction throughout his life, Barry embraced and mastered a comprehensive, critical approach to architecture, landscape, interiors, integrated sustainability, and teaching. If you speak with his clients, colleagues, and students, you will get a sense of one of the best architects and educators of any generation.

The real significance of Barry's contribution to Canadian architecture came home to me some years ago when I visited the Butterfly Conservatory with my children. We approached the elegant, chrysalis-like steel and glass enclosure emerging from the stone base. Upon entering the pavilion, we were delighted and filled with wonder seeing the diversity of butterflies fluttering and perching everywhere. In the wings of these butterflies, the inspiration for Barry's vision's design and meaning was revealed.

During the pandemic, Barry presented, on Zoom, the design concept for the new Robotics building at the University of Toronto Mississauga campus to the Design Review Committee. I saw right away that Barry's vision for this research and workspace for robotics shared the same qualities of the Butterfly Conservatory: elegant, efficient, and sustainable. Barry had let me know this would be his last building. Both are deeply grounded in their natural forest settings, and both have symbolically shaped roofs that give a distinct identity and expression to their respective programs. Similar to the Butterfly Conservatory, Barry envisioned a one-storey pavilion for the Robotics building. The roof will be an inverted light wood truss structure with cantilevered extensions on all sides. It seemed to me that Barry's proposal to create a unique geometric form integrating the warmth of the wood and emphasizing transparency held a more profound purpose: to remind the users of the implications of their work on Nature, and all life.

One of the gifts of this pandemic has been the series of phone conversations Barry and I were able to have over the last nine months. We talked about everything and everybody who had influenced us. We spoke of our formative years at the University of Toronto during a moment of significant change and disruption of the status quo in the late 1960s. We reminisced about our shared work experiences with George Baird, John van Nostrand, Joost Bakker, and Donald McKay during the 1970s. We laughed about the "crisis" of post-modernism in architecture in the 1980s and how it challenged us to reclaim meaning in architecture during the 1990s. We shared ideas and philosophies about integrating deep, sustainable, and interdisciplinary thinking with the art of architecture to create social benefit for the 21st century. We talked about our families and children and compared our personal experiences with cancer. Most of all, I feel grateful that I had the opportunity to express my gratitude to Barry and to tell him how much I valued our life-long friendship.

One of the last things I shared with Barry was a book, *the Architect on the Beach*.[1] It is about Le Corbusier's radical shift from creating architecture as "machines for living" to organic form-making, and how a collection of seashells ultimately led to the design of Ronchamp.

As a friend and an architect, I will always remember Barry leading the way, quietly, exploring the deeper meaning of sustainability long before the world began to pay attention to climate change. When architecture forgot its connection to Nature, Barry was quietly setting the groundwork for remembering.

Dear Barry, I am going to miss you, your ideas, and our conversations.

Donald McKay

Barry Sampson, the teacher

Barry Sampson: over 40 years a teacher, rising through the ranks from sessional lecturer to full professor for the last 15 years of his academic career. And in all that time, an architect – for 30 years of them as a partner – in a critical and celebrated architectural practice.

For a high school season, I was a member of the wrestling team. I enjoyed it, even if, tall and thin, I was unsuited to it. By necessity, I learned to assess other people as wrestlers. The first time I saw Barry Sampson, I recognized a natural wrestler. That was 53 years ago last September.

A wrestler's first inclination: stay in balance, take a broad stance and train to hold the ground. That is a place where Barry thrived. He studied conscientiously and widely, and he embodied what he learned, applying it to his own work and sharing it with colleagues and students, always developing the gravity he needed to ground the work. Teaching in parallel but never together, over the years I enjoyed reviewing student work with Barry. Characteristically, he would open his comments citing three or four principles or issues. You understood, when he spoke, he drew these from a bindle sack of dozens and dozens of such principles, developed in theory and practice and applied daily to test their value in teaching and in the office.

Wrestlers train, mastering fundamental positions, and dozens of moves from those positions. They seem solid, but they are quick, and will surprise an opponent in an act of recoupage. All of Barry's preparations, and a natural thoughtfulness, would lead him to a well-considered practice, but it does not mean he was unprepared for a change. After some consideration, however brief, he would always step in. His constant study and self-criticism gave him the leverage to advance the work when he understood where to apply the appropriate force, and what direction it should take.

Over his career, Barry's natural inclinations put him at the centre of two teaching streams.

For a decade and a half – until the century turned – he was a foundation figure in first-year studios in the School of Architecture, where new students learn so much so quickly. In the emotionally chaotic environment of those first years, he was a steadying influence, not only in the programs he developed, addressing the architectural craft step-by-step, but in his nature – benevolent and compassionate and profoundly professional.

And, for at least a dozen years in the new century, in Daniels' graduate program, he took responsibility for the comprehensive building studio, the exhaustive term-long exercise that draws on the full range of building skills and architectural gifts. It was a studio he prepared for, and renewed for himself, all his life.

And, in all that time, he never neglected his own self-development. Barry kept a place in his career for special studios, teaching from out of his own enthusiasms: for building in glass, for green building, and for educational institutions.

Unlike boxers, wrestlers are part of a team; the success of all is as important as the triumphs of one. Barry served his entire community in a wide range of ways, but most particularly, at the University of Toronto he nurtured two school buildings, seeing that each met the demands of the day while anticipating the future in architecture. Handled badly, this can be a thankless responsibility, and the gratitude of that school community for what he accomplished there is the best evidence of the depth of his contribution.

Good teachers leave behind an intellectual and moral DNA of sorts. Barry set a high mark for grace and integrity, for all of us. Generations of architects will, by his example, strive to meet it.

John van Nostrand

Barry Sampson, the professional

We were all in first year at the School of Architecture in Toronto – beginning in '67 and heading for graduation in '72. We were all "from away" – Bruce Kuwabara and I from Hamilton; Joost Bakker from Curacao; Donald McKay from Manitoba (via Etobicoke); and Barry from Oshawa.

Barry and I bonded early after I asked him what he had submitted as his portfolio. He took me over to his desk and pulled out his coloured drawings of new cars, including the hottest cars of the period: Corvettes, GTOs, Camaros. They were precisely drawn and rendered in beautiful metallic colours. This left me pondering for another 40 years over whether cars were more important in our times than buildings (we had all visited Expo '67). They were "modern" in ways that most of the kids our age in Oshawa and Hamilton understood: Hamilton sent much of its scrap steel from ancient cars back to GM, where they made new models. We all knew that a driver's license was our "ticket to ride," and was preferably obtained within a week of turning 16, if you were really cool. Barry was really cool.

In 1967, the school of architecture at the University of Toronto had undergone a major change in leadership, under the guidance of John Andrews. He invited Peter Prangnell (from England) to move from Columbia University to the University of Toronto, to serve as the new Director of Architecture.

Peter had strong affiliations with Team X (Team Ten) – a breakaway group including figures such as Aldo van Eyck that challenged the modernist founders of CIAM, including Le Corbusier. Team X formed in 1953 as a new global international organization focused on architecture that addressed the everyday needs of real people. They were interested in the ordinariness of everyday life, the house-as-city and city-as-house, the primitive Dogon with their squares that became circles. A weekly series of lectures led by Peter left us all in awe and confusion. We were asked to take our cameras out on the street to document this life – including "places where people gossiped," or "places that supported human action and emotion" – and to try to tell our classmates what we had each seen. We were told we already had 18 years of experiencing buildings and cities, and that we needed to bring that experience to our work.

In '69, Peter invited George Baird to the school. George had just returned from several years in London, where he had co-edited *Meaning & Architecture* with Charles Jencks,[1] a book which introduced us to a completely new set of ideas, starting with "semiology:"

> *...the justification for semiology, the theory of signs... contends that since everything is meaningful, we are in a literal sense condemned to meaning, and thus we can either become aware of how meaning works in a technical sense (semiology), or we can remain content with our intuition.*

From that point on, we lived in the midst of this juxtaposition of theory (George) with intuition and emotion (Peter). This was a situation in which Barry thrived. And with the subsequent establishment of George Baird Architect in 1972, it went beyond talking and "thinking and jumping" to projects – fascinating projects.

A student of Barry's (who later became my business partner) recounted an experience from his thesis year. He selected Barry as his advisor and met with him at least once a week, and then twice as it got closer to the final review. Without fail, Barry would always end their meetings with a summary of his critique, telling him that it was not coming together, it lacked rigour, and that he needed to get his ideas and their outcome together, and so on. Then, after the formal presentation to an assembled set of peers and professors, Barry took him aside and told him it was a "pretty good" project that got its point across. Barry would go on to recommend him to some well-known practices in the USA and Europe.

Barry demanded perfection: of himself first, and then everyone else. Ignoring Robert Frost, he took two paths at once – one as teacher and the other as practitioner. It was a model that few of the five of us could handle: as both an exceptional teacher and someone who led the creation of exceptional buildings. Barry was both a social architect and a social activist (a whole other story). He was at the centre of both the city and its industrial and economic hubs.

With affection, we nicknamed him "Blue Barry." When he looked gloomy, he was really just turning everything over, and over, and over again. He got it right, any way that you turn it.

Joost Bakker

Barry Sampson, the global community member

People enter into our lives, even if only for a brief number of years, and form markers that reverberate throughout our life.

I was last with Barry, and our original "hopeful circle" in Toronto, September 5, 2019. It was exactly 52 years ago to that day when this circle of friends/colleagues entered architecture school at U of T! We were gathered around that familiar dining room table at George and Elizabeth Baird's, reminiscing and celebrating – Barry, John van Nostrand, Bruce Kuwabara, Donald McKay, and our partners.

On day one of school, our circle was confined to De Stijl-like exercises: composing cut-out grey shapes on white cardstock. Within short months, we were suddenly unleashed into the tumultuous '60s and '70s, and empowering new design thinking deeply rooted in ideas of community. I have largely witnessed Barry's unfolding from afar, having moved to Vancouver in 1974. From this vantage point, I have come to realize how deeply rooted Barry remained in "community" – as person, professional, and educator.

> *To travel far, far – and that first morning's awakening under a new sky!*
> *And to find oneself in it – no, to discover more of oneself there.*
> *—Rainer Maria Rilke*[1]

A Volkswagen van road trip in 1971 to Latin America uncovered another transformative awakening in our lives. Meeting up with Barry, John, Danny McAlister, and Norm Grey-Noble in Panama City, we took our VW/home to Buenaventura on Colombia's Pacific Coast. The resonance of that trip stays with us to this day. We encountered a deep multilayered history with diverse cultural expressions and senses of public space, discovering a radically different world.

Together, we explored barridas on the mudflats of Buenaventura. We witnessed "Inti Raymi" – the ancient Inca festival of the Sun – in late June with bonfires proliferating on surrounding hills. We danced on the dark side of the moon with Pink Floyd blaring from a camped van's roof in a seemingly endless Peruvian desert. We drove through devastated small villages and the town of Huaraz, places that had fallen victim of the Ancash earthquake the previous year.

For Barry, this trip awakened themes of lifelong interest, including a lasting love of travel. His travels and inquiries continued throughout the '70s, with studies in London, sojourns to Paris, and studies at the Sorbonne.

Over the ensuing decades, Barry crossed this country extensively while working on projects, design competitions, exhibitions, and urban studies. His firm's 1982 "Greening Downtown" urban design study continues to define Vancouver's Georgia Street, our main ceremonial street. My collaboration with Barry, George Baird and Donald McKay remains memorable.

> *[Ursula Franklin] defined technology as practice: how things are socially and morally done. She saw technology as complex systems of methods, procedures and mindsets rather than a collection of machines and gadgets.*[2]

A life immersed in travel, study, building, education, and family allowed Barry to excel as an insightful and holistic teacher of practice. The inter-connectedness of environmental and architectural systems eventually led to a new mindset and focus on "bioclimatic" design. As a young colleague (and University of Toronto grad) in my office reminisced: "Barry's comprehensive building studio – weaving together structures, envelope and sustainability, acoustics, lighting sources and more – was a student favorite, particularly for those interested in architecture as a practice for designing and constructing buildings… something that sometimes gets lost in academia."

> *I thought of the cottage as more of my home than the family home in Oshawa. I just felt I belonged there.*
> *—Barry Sampson*[3]

The deepest and strongest root running through Barry's life was his cottage in Haliburton. This faux-log structure was hand-built by his father at the end of the Second World War. There was growing pressure to renew this small aging structure and meet the needs of multiple generations. That offered Barry the opportunity to reflect on, and conceive of, a high-performance all-season space that fully expressed his lifelong values.

His father's original timber cottage is now lovingly suspended and encased within a state-of-the-art sustainable glass enclosure. This transformed place on Beech Lake will remain a wonderful testament to Barry's life and learnings, his sense of belonging, while providing ongoing community for his partner Judi and their sons.

Sampson Cottage

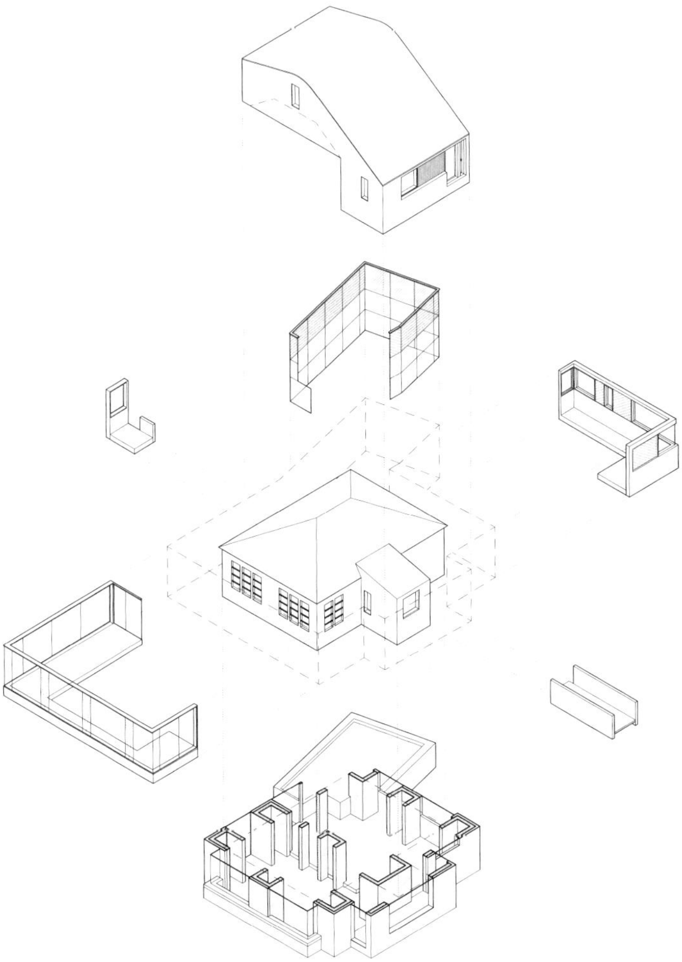

Barry Sampson was a highly regarded and audacious architect, not so much because he took extreme positions or risks, but rather because of his ability to take on a broad range of issues simultaneously. This inclination rendered exceptional results, as the cottage on Beech Lake that he designed and built for his family illustrates.

Barry's father built the original 750 square foot cabin for his family in 1950. This little cabin held a significant place in Barry's heart as a vessel of family memory. As time passed, the minimal structure – sited at the base of a small cliff and subject to significant surface water runoff – began to deteriorate. Clearly a substantial rebuild or replacement was required, and Barry, true to his nature, embraced the challenge as an opportunity to explore his fundamental architectural values: a reverence for history, a desire to accommodate the complexities of a multigenerational user group, a commitment to sustainability, and the need to express these divergent objectives architecturally. This inclusive approach was not something new to Barry; rather, it was simply the way he rolled.

He called the design response "Cottage Wrap." The existing cabin was treated as an artifact, clearly legible within the composition of the new building and raised on steel beams to get it out of the wet ground. This strategy provides space for a lower level, configured in plan using U-shaped concrete piers upon which the steel lifting beams are supported. The concrete structure provides thermal mass for the building and additional living space to accommodate family members and friends. The cottage is now entered from the arrival/parking area via a bridge that leads to the raised public living space. The axis of the bridge extends through the building as an armature of circulation, grazes the back of the central hearth, and culminates with a view of the shoreline and lake beyond.

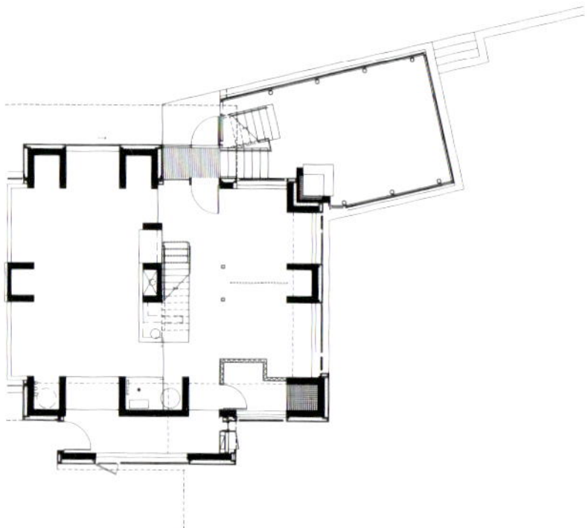

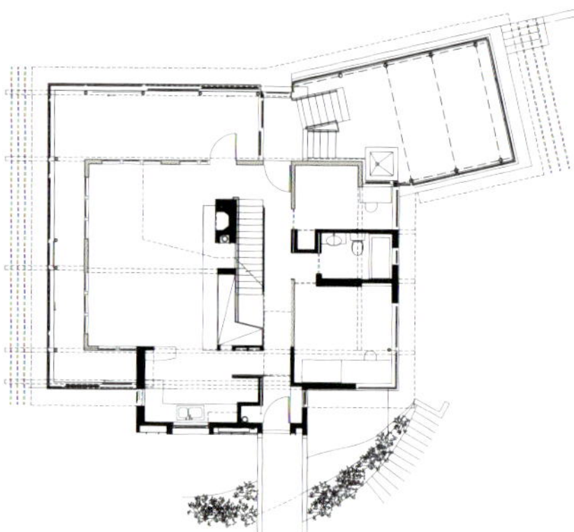

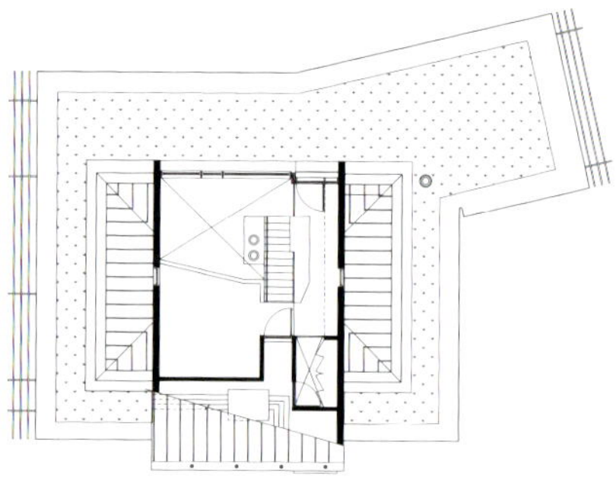

On this elevated level, one can experience the rich history of the inner realm of the original cabin, and enjoy the juxtaposition of its minimal single glazed windows in relation to the new high-performance lift-and-slide glazed wrap. Both of these glazing systems make a valuable contribution to the character of the space, with the super transparency of the wrap complementing the intimate containment provided by the old cabin. From this raised level, the site is experienced differently. The views are more contained by the trees on the periphery of the property, and the view frame from each window edits out the middle ground so that one's relationship to the site requires the engagement of the imagination, resulting in a more compelling and personal experience of the landscape. A lofty screened-in porch enjoys a view of the waterfront. At a level halfway between the principal rooms and the new lower level, this porch celebrates the experience of minimal boundaries between an important place of inhabitation and nature. A loft above the artifact cabin provides a generous master bedroom and a grand view to the water.

On a small cottage project such at this, most architects would attempt to reduce the number of concepts driving the design so that they could have more control over a minimum number of essential ideas. Barry Sampson's optimism and commitment to ideas prevented him from doing this. With a modest budget, he sought to resolve the complex range of issues as he saw them and refused to diminish the significance or influence of any of them. The resultant cottage is richer and more powerful for this way of working.

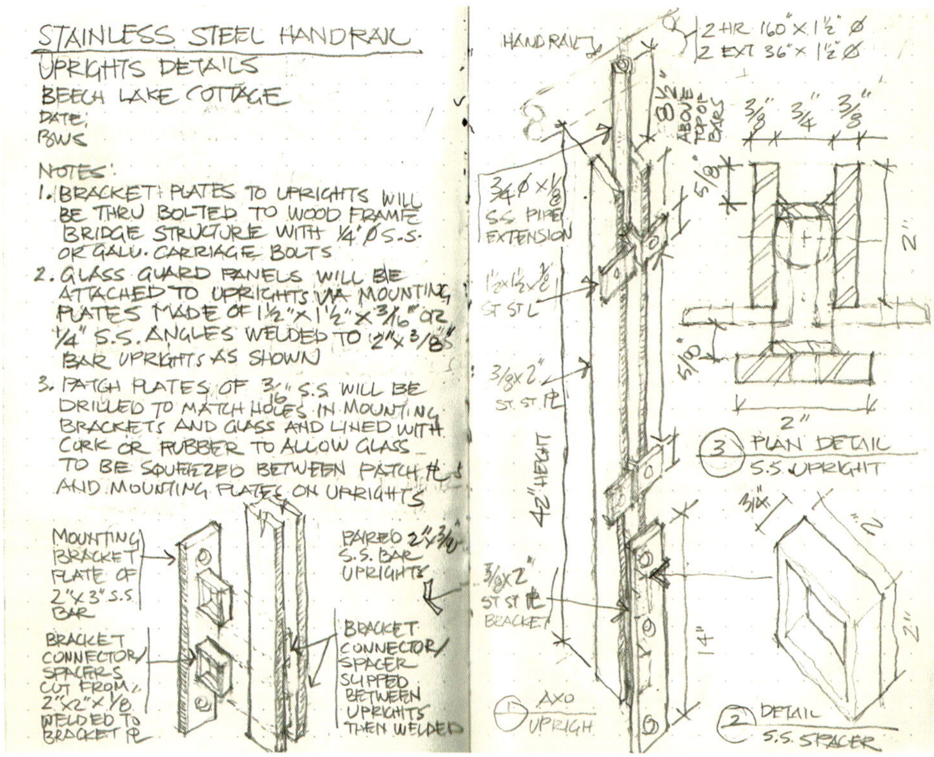

STAINLESS STEEL HANDRAIL
UPRIGHTS DETAILS
BEECH LAKE COTTAGE
DATE:
BWS
NOTES:
1. BRACKET PLATES TO UPRIGHTS WILL BE THRU BOLTED TO WOOD FRAME BRIDGE STRUCTURE WITH 1/4" Ø S.S. OR GALV. CARRIAGE BOLTS
2. GLASS GUARD PANELS WILL BE ATTACHED TO UPRIGHTS VIA MOUNTING PLATES MADE OF 1½"x1½"x3/16" OR 1/4" S.S. ANGLES WELDED TO 2"x3/8" BAR UPRIGHTS AS SHOWN
3. PATCH PLATES OF 3/16" S.S WILL BE DRILLED TO MATCH HOLES IN MOUNTING BRACKETS AND GLASS AND LINED WITH CORK OR RUBBER TO ALLOW GLASS TO BE SQUEEZED BETWEEN PATCH PL AND MOUNTING PLATES ON UPRIGHTS
MOUNTING BRACKET PLATE OF 2"x3" S.S. BAR
BRACKET CONNECTOR/ SPACERS CUT FROM 2"x2"x1/8 WELDED TO BRACKET PL
PAIRED 2"x3/8" S.S. BAR UPRIGHTS
BRACKET CONNECTOR/ SPACER SLIPPED BETWEEN UPRIGHTS THEN WELDED
HANDRAIL
2 HR 160"x1½" Ø
2 EXT 36"x1½" Ø
3/4 Ø x 1/8 S.S. PIPE EXTENSION
1½x1½x3/16 ST ST L
3/8x2" ST ST PL
42" HEIGHT
3/8x2" ST ST PL BRACKET
14"
1 AXO UPRIGHT
3 PLAN DETAIL S.S. UPRIGHT
2 DETAIL S.S. SPACER

Contributors

George Baird is Emeritus Professor and former Dean of the John H. Daniels Faculty of Architecture, Landscape, and Design at the University of Toronto, and founding principal of Baird Sampson Neuert architects. His publications include *Meaning in Architecture* (with Charles Jencks); *Alvar Aalto; The Space of Appearance; Public Space: Cultural/Political Theory; Street Photography;* and *Writings on Architecture and the City.* A collection of essays and interviews devoted to his work, *The Architect and the Public* edited by Roberto Damiani, was published in 2020. He received the 2010 RAIC Gold Medal and the 2012 Topaz Medallion of the AIA/ACSA. In 2016, he was invested in the Order of Canada.

Joost Bakker is a founding partner of DIALOG in Vancouver. Born in Curaçao, he is a fourth-generation architect in his family. For over 45 years, he has brought strong urbanist values to his professional, artistic, and volunteer work. Pioneering work on the internationally recognized redevelopment of Granville Island, university projects, and the Royal Canadian Navy Monument reflect the diversity and creativity of his practice. In 2017 he received the AIBC Lifetime Achievement Award, and is a dauntless volunteer to numerous civic, arts, and cultural organizations in Vancouver. He is a Fellow of the Royal Architectural Institute of Canada and a member of the Royal Canadian Academy of Arts.

David Bowick, a structural engineer, is a principal of Blackwell Engineering, where he has worked since 1990. A three-time recipient of the WoodWorks Building the Future engineering award, he has received recognition for his work in wood, concrete, and steel, and has worked on numerous projects across Canada that have received architectural awards. An Adjunct Professor in the Master of Architecture program at the University of Toronto, he is a member of the Canadian Standards Association Technical Committee on CAN/CSA-O86, Engineering Design in Wood, and the Technical Committee responsible for the Engineering Guide for Wood Frame Construction.

Bruce Kuwabara is a founding partner of KPMB Architects and Chair of the Board of Trustees of the Canadian Centre for Architecture. As the design partner for numerous award-winning KPMB projects, he played a central role in notable buildings, including Richmond City Hall, the National Ballet School, Boston University Data Sciences Centre, Manitoba Hydro Place, and the winning design in the 2020 international competition for the Art Gallery of Nova Scotia. He serves as a critic, lecturer, and spokesperson for architectural excellence in the shaping of equitable, sustainable, and vibrant cities and communities. He was awarded the RAIC Gold Medal in 2006 and is an Officer of the Order of Canada.

Ian MacDonald is the principal of Ian MacDonald Architect, Inc. Following architectural studies at the University of Waterloo and Carleton University, he worked with John Parkin, Ron Thom, and Arthur Erickson before establishing his own office in 1984. He taught at the University of Toronto from 1984 to 2000. His work has been widely recognized and published internationally. He has received three Governor General's Medals in Architecture and numerous awards from the OAA and the RAIC. The monograph *boundary sequence illlusion: Ian MacDonald Architect* was published by Dalhousie Architectural Press in 2019. He is a Fellow of the Royal Architectural Institute of Canada.

Donald McKay is Professor Emeritus of Architecture at the University of Waterloo and principal of Donald McKay studio. During his 40 years of teaching McKay led a series of planning teams, and designed and built small buildings, furniture, and exhibitions, including The Evidence Room, shown at the 2016 Venice Bienniale. He is currently preparing a photographic atlas of Père Lachaise Cemetery in Paris and completing several book projects, including *The Chess Game: exile, sculpture, photography, and chess in the Twentieth Century.*

Jon Neuert is a principal of Baird Sampson Neuert where, over a period of 30 years, he has played a key role in the design of prominent cultural and tourism projects, ranging from the Butterfly Conservatory and the French River Visitor Centre to recent work on the Mission 2050 agri-ecology campus. With a background in science and architecture, his work is focused on the social and environmental opportunities of sustainable design. An active community volunteer, he was appointed by Toronto City Council to its Community Environmental Assessment Team (CEAT) and served as chair of CEAT's Technology and Research Subcommittee. He is a Fellow of the Royal Architectural Institute of Canada.

Erik Olsen is a managing partner at Transsolar KlimaEngineering, an international climate engineering firm that focuses on the design of exceptional, highly comfortable spaces with a positive environmental impact. He leads the New York team in working collaboratively with architects worldwide to develop and validate low-energy, architecturally-integrated climate and energy concepts. He is committed to innovation that adds value to the human experience. In addition to his specialist work at Transsolar, he has worked as a consulting mechanical engineer on a wide variety of building types. He launched and directed the City of Chicago's Green Permit Program.

Pina Petricone is an Associate Professor at the John H. Daniels Faculty of Architecture, Landscape, and Design, and a founding principal of Giannone Petricone Associates Architects. Her research, teaching, and design practice are built around questions of tectonics, identity, and material expression with capacity to assume cultural voices in architecture and city-making. Her work has been published widely in Canada, the US, Asia, and Europe. A current speculative design project, "Boundaries of Difference: The Toronto Party Wall Project," traces the durability of the party wall in old, renovated, and new constructions across culturally-specific neighbourhoods. She is a Fellow of the Royal Architectural Institute of Canada.

Brigitte Shim is a Professor at the John H. Daniels Faculty of Architecture, Landscape, and Design. She has held a series of distinguished visiting professorships and has served on international, national, and local design juries and committees as an advocate for design excellence. With Howard Sutcliffe, she is a founding principal of Shim Sutcliffe Architects, whose work has received numerous Canadian and international awards and has been widely published. She is a Fellow of the Royal Architectural Institute of Canada. In 2013, Shim and Sutcliffe were awarded the Order of Canada, and they are the recipients of the 2021 RAIC Gold Medal.

Richard Sommer is a Professor of Architecture and Urbanism and director of the Global Cities Institute at the University of Toronto, where he was Dean of the Daniels Faculty from 2009 to 2020. He was formerly the Director of Urban Design at Harvard University's Graduate School of Design and held several visiting professorships and fellowships in Europe and the US. His projects and writings on monument-making, architecture, and urbanism have been published in *Cabinet Magazine, Perspecta,* the *Journal of Architectural Education,* and in books including *Urban Design* and *Commemoration and the American City: Monuments, Memorialization, and Meaning,* among others.

Nader Tehrani is Dean of The Irwin S. Chanin School of Architecture at The Cooper Union in New York City and previously served as Head of Architecture at MIT from 2010 to 2014. He is a founding principal of NADAAA, a Boston-based practice dedicated to the advancement of design innovation, interdisciplinary collaboration, and an intensive dialogue with the construction industry. The work of NADAAA has been widely published and exhibited, and has received numerous awards. In 2020, Tehrani received the American Academy of Arts and Letters' Arnold W. Brunner Memorial Prize for his contributions to architecture as an art and, in 2021, was appointed as a member of the Academy.

John van Nostrand is a founding partner of SvN Architects + Planners. Since 1974, he has directed the firm's architectural, planning, and urban design practices. SvN focuses on the integration of housing, land development, and infrastructure in cities and landscapes undergoing constant growth and renewal. His work and writings have received recognition at home and abroad, including the World Leadership Award for Town Planning, the Daniel Burnham Award from the American Planning Association, and numerous local and national awards. In 2004, he received the Jane Jacobs Prize. He is a Fellow of the Royal Architectural Institute of Canada.

Robert Wright is an Associate Professor and Interim Dean of the John H. Daniels Faculty of Architecture, Landscape, and Design, former Chair of the Landscape Program, and principal of iz, an exploratory design practice. As an educator and design practitioner, he believes that design is built theory, and that the translation from concept to built works is essential to design discourse. With training in both ecology and landscape architecture, he views design as the interplay of nature, person, community, city, and place. His practice seeks collaborative experimentation in architecture, landscape architecture, and urban design as well as fashion, furniture, art, and industrial arts.

Brian Carter, a graduate of the Nottingham School of Architecture and the University of Toronto, is a registered architect who worked in practice with Arup in London prior to his appointment as Chair of Architecture at the University of Michigan. He was subsequently appointed Dean of the School of Architecture and Planning at the University at Buffalo, The State University of New York where he is currently Professor of Architecture. Elected a Fellow of the Royal Society of Arts in 1992, he was appointed an Honorary Fellow of the Royal Architectural Institute of Canada in 2017.

Annette LeCuyer trained at the Architectural Association in London and is a registered architect in the United Kingdom. She is a Professor in the School of Architecture and Planning at the University at Buffalo, The State University of New York, where her work focuses on the integration of design and construction in contemporary architecture. She is author of *Radical Tectonics; Steel and Beyond – New Strategies for Metals in Architecture;* and *ETFE – Technology and Design*. Elected as a Fellow of the Royal Society of Arts in 1999, she was appointed an Honorary Fellow of the Royal Architectural Institute of Canada in 2017.

Christian Unverzagt is a founding partner and design director of M1DTW, a multidisciplinary studio engaged in expanding the boundaries of practice through the design of objects, artifacts, identities, and spaces. A graduate of SCI-Arc, he is an Associate Professor of Practice in Architecture at the University of Michigan Taubman College of Architecture and Urban Planning. M1DTW has won five AIA Michigan Honor Awards since 2015, and books they have designed have received awards from the AIA and the American Institute of Graphic Arts. *Working in Mumbai* – a book documenting the work of Rahul Mehrotra/RMA Architects – was designed by M1DTW and published in 2020 by ArchiTangle in Berlin.

Endnotes

Richard Sommer Introduction

1 Le Corbusier, *Creation is a Patient Search* (New York: Frederick A. Praeger, 1960).

Barry Sampson Questions of Practice

1 Jean-Jacques Rousseau, *Rousseau, Judge of Jean-Jacques, Dialogues,* ed. Roger D. Masters and Christopher Kelly, trans. Judith R. Bush, Christopher Kelly, and Roger D. Masters (Hanover: University Press of New England, 1990).

Jean-Jacques Rousseau, *The Confessions and Correspondence, Including the Letters to Malesherbes,* ed. Christopher Kelly, Roger D. Masters, and Peter G. Stillman, trans. Christopher Kelly (Hanover: University Press of New England, 1995).

Jean-Jacques Rousseau, *The Reveries of the Solitary Walker,* trans. Charles E. Butterworth (New York: New York University Press, 1979).

2 Alvar Aalto, George Baird, and Yukio Futagawa, *Alvar Aalto* (New York: Simon and Schuster, 1971).

3 Kenneth Frampton, "Maison De Verre," *Perspecta,* vol. 12 (1969), 77–128.

4 Rem Koolhaas, Madelon Vreisendorp, Elia Zenghelis, and Zoe Zenghelis, "Exodus, or the voluntary prisoners of architecture," thesis presented at the Architectural Association School of Architecture in London (1972).

5 James Lorimer and Evelyn Ross, eds., *The City Book: The Planning and Politics of Canada's Cities* (Toronto: J. Lorimer, 1976).

6 George Baird and Barry Sampson, "Main Street: Can it Survive the Shopping Centre?," ed. James Lorimer and Carolyn MacGregor, *After the Developers* (Toronto: J. Lorimer, 1981).

7 Walter Benjamin, "The Work of Art in the Age of Mechanical Reproduction," *Illuminations: Essays and Reflections,* ed. Hannah Arendt and trans. Harry Zohn (New York: Schocken Books, 1969), 18.

8 Barry Sampson, "Reframing," in *boundary sequence illusion: Ian MacDonald Architect* (Halifax: Dalhousie Architectural Press, 2019), 8.

9 Gemma Tipton, "Why are Irish world class architects not building in Ireland?" *Irish Times,* 9 October 2019.

10 Jean-Jacques Rousseau, *The Reveries of the Solitary Walker,* trans. Charles E. Butterworth (New York: New York University Press, 1979), 253.

Thomas L. Wells Public School

1 Nadav Malin, "Case Study Revisit—Thomas L. Wells Public School," *Greensource Magazine,* March 2011.

Jon Neuert

1 See Detlef Mertins, "The Enticing and Threatening Face of Prehistory: Walter Benjamin and the Utopia of Glass," *Assemblage 29* (April 1996), 6–23.

Robert Wright

1 F. Hamilton Hazlehurst, *Gardens of Illusion: the Genius of André Le Nostre* (Nashville: Vanderbilt University Press, 1980).

Ian MacDonald

1 Barry Sampson, "Reframing," *boundary sequence illusion: Ian MacDonald Architect* (Halifax: Dalhousie Architectural Press, 2019), 6–9.

Bruce Kuwabara

1 Niklas Mak, *Le Corbusier: the Architect on the Beach* (Munich: Hirmer Verlag, 2011).

John van Nostrand

1 Charles Jencks and George Baird, eds., *Meaning in Architecture* (New York: George Braziller, 1970).

Joost Bakker

1 Rainer Maria Rilke, letter to a friend, 3 February, 1923.

2 See Ursula Franklin, *The Real World of Technology* (Toronto: Anansi, 1999), revised edition.

3 Barry Sampson, quoted in *Cottage Life,* 4 May, 2020.

Image Credits

All images, unless otherwise noted, supplied by/credited to Baird Sampson Neuert architects.

Tom Arban: 40, 41, 43, 48, 67 lower left, 70, 78, 82, 83, 84, 86, 87, 89.
Michael Awad: 32.
George Baird: 14 center + right, 16 lower, 27 lower left; 16 upper left/courtesy of Thames & Hudson Ltd., London.
BSN/MBTW: 23 lower.
BSN/Tony Scherman: 30 upper.
Canadian Architectural Archives/courtesy of Judi Coburn: 27 upper.
Canadian Centre for Architecture:
Ivan Leonidov Film Studio: 19 lower right.
James Stirling/Michael Wilford fonds: 20, 26 right.
Kenneth Frampton fonds/gift of Kenneth Frampton: 17 upper left + right.
Harry Choi: 10, 12, 24, 34, 46, 58.
Don Cochran: 53.
John H. Daniels Faculty of Architecture, Landscape and Design: 94 right, 95.
Hans Jan Durr: 19 upper, 21 upper left.
Richard Einzig/Arcaid: 26 upper left.
Steven Evans: 31, 39.
Fondation Le Corbusier/Art Resource: 42 right.
Debbie Franke: 57.
Michael Halberstadt/Arcaid: 17 lower left.
Emilia Hurd/BSN: 65 lower.
Bruce Kuwabara: 15 left, 21 right.
Jim Leier: 15 right.
James Lorimer & Company Ltd, Publishers: 22, 23 upper.
Paul Orenstein: 71 right, 118 lower, 121, 123.
Steven Park/courtesy of Princeton Architectural Press; SOCAN/ Fondation Le Corbusier: 21 lower left.
Pictoright/SOCAN/courtesy of A.W. Bruna, Utrecht: 18 right, 19 lower left.
Stijn Poelstra/collection Centraal Museum, Utrecht: 18 left.
Barry Sampson/courtesy of Judi Coburn: 72 left, 90, 118 upper left + upper right, 119, 120, 122 lower.
Richard Seck: 36, 37 upper, 38 upper left + right, 65 middle left + right, 66, 71 lower left, 122 upper left + right.
Peter A. Sellar: 61.
Lawrence Speck: 16 upper right.
James Stirling: 26 lower left.
Geoffrey Taunton/Alamy: 42 left.
Terence Tourangeau: 45, 52 upper right, 62.

Every reasonable attempt has been made to identify owners of copyright. Errors or omissions will be corrected in subsequent editions.

Acknowledgements

This book, an initiative by colleagues of Barry Sampson, documents his significant contributions to architectural practice and the education of architects. These contributors have shaped the project through their thoughtful words – words that recognize an architect whole-heartedly committed to design, its potential to integrate ideas and improve lives.

The book has been made possible by the support of the University of Toronto's John H. Daniels Faculty of Architecture, Landscape and Design. Professor and Interim Dean Robert Wright and Professor Richard Sommer have played vital roles, together with Brigitte Shim and Bruce Kuwabara. Judi Coburn's assistance has been essential in realizing this book. Ian MacDonald's contributions, including the Sampson Cottage text, are greatly appreciated.

Nene Brode has provided invaluable administrative support. Alexandra Ntoukas – a patient, thoughtful, and perceptive research assistant – worked tirelessly to source images, obtain permissions, seek out drawings, and chase down references – complex tasks at any time, and made all the more challenging by the uncertainties of this particular moment.

The Baird Lecture was given by Barry Sampson on October 24, 2019 at the University of Toronto. We are especially grateful to Jon Neuert, George Baird, and staff at Baird Sampson Neuert for providing images and information, and supporting this publication. The contributions of photographers who documented the work of Barry Sampson and Baird Sampson Neuert are invaluable.

Many institutions and individuals have provided assistance: Martien de Vletter and Caroline Dagbert at the Canadian Centre for Architecture in Montreal; the Canadian Architectural Archives in Calgary; SOCAN; Diana Edkins at Art Resource; Joe Weston at Princeton Architectural Press; Steven Atkinson at Arcaid; Lisa Doherty at the Eberhard Zeidler Library at University of Toronto; Courtney Morshed at the School of Architecture at University of Texas at Austin; and Rose Orcutt of University at Buffalo Libraries. Elsa Lam, the editor of *Canadian Architect,* generously allowed the tributes to Barry Sampson, first published in the December 20, 2020 issue of that journal, to be reprinted.

The Board of Dalhousie Architectural Press responded enthusiastically to the book proposal and moved quickly to support its publication. Susanne Marshall's advice has been extremely helpful in refining ideas and managing the process.

Particular thanks are due to Christian Unverzagt of M1DTW for his thoughtful design, careful preparation, and patient oversight of printing.

We are grateful for the enthusiastic efforts of all who have participated in this celebration of the life and work of Barry Sampson – a notable architect, respected teacher, and an inspiration to so many.

Annette LeCuyer & Brian Carter